Half a

The Realist's Guide™

BLOOMING TWIG BOOKS / NEW YORK, NY

Bill,
Have a great conference!
IPMA-HR 2011

Half a Glass: The Realist's Guide™

Copyright ©2010 Craig Price

www.therealistsguide.com

www.speakercraigprice.com

877-572-7890

281-546-1664

Published by:

Blooming Twig Books

PO Box 4668 #66675

New York, NY 10163-4668

1-866-389-1482

www.bloomingtwig.com

ISBN 978-1-933918-60-0

First Edition, First Printing

9 8 7 6 5 4 3 2 1

Dedication

To my wife, Heather.

I'd be lost without you.
Mostly, because you have the directions in your purse...
I love you more than anything!

{ Table of Contents

Half a Glass

The Realist's Guide™

RULES FROM
THE REALIST

WHATEVER YOU THINK THIS BOOK IS ABOUT, YOU'RE WRONG.

This was not written by some veneered, spray-tanned, pseudo-science touting, Tony Robbins wanna-be, who has the "the secret" about life, money and success.

This isn't some new age, spiritual journey towards enlightenment that will shake the very bedrock of your beliefs. There is none of that "bullshistic" medicine to be found in here.[1]

This isn't a book where I delve into some horrible situations in my past, only to show how I made it a positive, wonderful, sunshiny spectacle. I've had a pretty good life so far, not much to complain about. Then again, I'm not the most positive person you'll ever meet, either. Yet somehow I, like millions of other realists out there, am doing pretty well for myself.

Hey, you bought this book, so that's a plus!

---

[1] "Bullshistic" being a cross between holistic and bullshit. Bullshistic medicine is the belief that crazy, untested, obviously ridiculous methods, nowhere close to being based on any science, are a valid treatment. Basically, its stuff that sounds hokey, unbelievable and that you only attempted because you ran out of real options and said "It can't hurt." True, it can't hurt, except it doesn't help either.

This is a "realist's" guide for a reason. The "real" I talk about is "reality", something many of the people spouting out answers nowadays forget. You know, the ones who say, "Quit your job and do what you want!" Easy for them to say. They make six figures a year and aren't the ones quitting their jobs. You, on the other hand, have a real life to keep going. Bills to pay, responsibilities to others. That doesn't mean you can't do or become what you want. It just means it takes a bit more work and planning.

Don't expect any of that "how to turn a frown upside down" crap from me.

I won't be showing you any *"secrets"*. Or telling you "If you *think* it, it will *happen*!" Really? I spent most of my teenage years thinking of Elle McPherson, yet she doesn't have a clue I exist.[2] Nor am I deluded into thinking I have a shot if we were to somehow meet. Especially now that I am married.[3]

The so-called "Law of Attraction" isn't a law, since it can easily be disproven. The Law of Attraction states that thoughts (both conscious and unconscious) dictate one's reality. Basically, if you think you're rich, you will be rich. If you think you're ill, you'll get ill. Plane crashes easily disprove this. Do you think more passengers on US Airways Flight 1549, as they were descending rather rapidly toward the Hudson River on January 15th, 2009, thought they were going to live or going to die? And if the majority thought they were going to die, did the few who thought they would make it just think harder than the others?

Want to get the *real* secret? Tell people what they *want* to hear and

---

[2] Hi, Elle!

[3] Hi, Honey!

not what they *need* to hear, have *no* proof or accountability, and just *watch* the money roll in.[4]

There are a lot of various programs and books out there that claim they can eliminate the negativity in your life. While they are all well-intentioned, they cannot deliver on that promise because negativity is a natural, ingrained thought process. You can't get rid of it. Not completely, anyway. Even if you are able to miraculously suppress all your negative thoughts, negative things will *still* happen to you. It would be like claiming that they could singlehandedly eliminate all sickness, war, and death from the world. It's just not possible.

If I'm not going to do any of those things, what is this book good for? A doorstop? Paperweight? A Christmas gift for the grouch down the hall?[5]

This book is a guide to show you how to get a grip on your negative thoughts, fears and doubts to use them to your advantage. Life isn't always going to go as planned, so we need to learn how to play the cards we're dealt, not hope and wish we had different cards. To *manage* negativity, you need to admit that it exists and that it's a part of life.

Negativity is realization of an unwanted outcome. It is worry, doubt, fear, skepticism, complaining, blame or any other acceptance of the fact that unwanted stuff happens.

How we deal with that "stuff" is the key.

---

[4] My tongue is in my cheek. As expected, it tastes cheeky.

[5] Personally, I like the last one myself. Feel free to buy as many copies as you can afford and then air-drop them onto the parking lot of your office!

Before you get started, here are a few ground rules to help you use this guide:

1. **It is not necessary to read the chapters in order.** Take a second to look back at the table of contents and if you so choose, flip to the section that interests you the most. This is not the Da Vinci Code. There is no plot, character arc or inane story of intrigue and convoluted clues to move you through to the next chapter. If you want, go from start to finish. Just don't feel obligated to do so. It's your book now, do with it as you'd like!

2. **You do not have to read this in one sitting.** There are going to be things in this book you don't agree with, other things you will whole-heartedly believe in and even other things that will make you put the book down for a second and say, "Hmm. I'm not sure I know what to think about that. That's new. I never looked at it that way." Use that time to think[6] about the validity, the application, or the consequences of anything you might read.

3. **You can defile this book.** Unless you checked this out of the library or borrowed it from someone else, feel free to highlight, underline, comment or even plain old vandalize the book. This book is intended to be a resource, a reference or possibly hollowed out to hide a weapon. It is not meant to be read and then put on the shelf or resold as some sort of collectible. Write, dog-ear, or tear out pages even. Whatever will help you use this the way that best suits you.

[6] Yes, you are going to have to think for yourself in this book. Isn't that refreshing?!

That's pretty much it.

I hope you enjoy the book. Laugh a little, learn something and maybe even see things from a new perspective.

Now get reading!

[7]

PRICE
PERSONALITY SCALE

This scale categorizes the various types of positive and negative personalities.

	DELUSIONAL POLLYANNA	1
1-3 is in the danger zone of being too positive for your own good.	**PRESCRIPTION MEDICATED**	2
	OPTIMIST	3
	POSITIVE THINKER	4
4-6 is the normal range. These are the most common personality types you'll encounter on a day to day basis.	**INDIFFERENT**	5
	NEGATIVE THINKER	6
	PESSIMIST	7
7-9 is the danger zone of being too negative and quite often is what people believe negative people are. As you can see by the scale, This is way past healthy.	**CLEANING THEIR GUNS**	8
	FATALISTIC DEPRESSIVE	9

Nothing can be wrong, nothing ever does go wrong, nothing ever will go wrong. These are the infuriating people who have no concept of reality but thankfully never obtain positions of influence or power. See holistic crystal worshipper, old pot head hippies, and self help gurus (ON-STAGE).

Whether under the influence of medication or not, this personality type seems like they are on some sort of anti-depressant. They see everything as rosy, although are unclear why. See Stepford Housewife.

Truly believes that the world cannot be all bad, always upbeat and certain that things will always go their way... even when evidence, concrete or anecdotal, proves otherwise. See Camp Counselor, Mortgage Broker/Stock Broker/Real Estate Agent (Circa 2005—2007).

Looks on the upside of most things. Tries to see silver linings instead of clouds. Occasionally has bad days, yet usually can find the advantages of any given situation.

I'd explain this but I just don't care enough.

Looks on the downside of most things while trying to create success. Always looks for potential problems and issues. Often is a pleasant, nice person, just has tendencies to think things through, plan and prepare.

Truly believes that the world isn't a happy rosy place and that most things will end in failure...even after they obtain success. See Life Insurance agents, mechanics, the French.

Worrying and wondering when the other shoe will drop, these types of people need constant observation. A bit paranoid, nothing ever seems to be going their way and failure is more the norm. See Internet Conspiracy theorists, weird dudes with three names (i.e. John Wilkes Booth, Lee Harvey Oswald) and employees at the DMV.

Nothing ever goes right, nothing ever has gone right, and nothing ever will go right. These are the truly baffling types of people who would rather talk than do. They complain about how bad things are, yet never seem willing to take any constructive action. See Serial killers, mental unbalanced individuals and self help gurus (OFF-STAGE).

INTRODUCTION

Half Empty or Half Full?

I'M SURE YOU'VE HEARD SOMEONE ASK THE PHILOSOPHICAL QUESTION "DO YOU LOOK AT A GLASS AS HALF EMPTY OR AS HALF FULL?" THE REALITY IS THIS: IT DOESN'T MATTER. EITHER WAY, YOU'RE LEFT WITH HALF A GLASS OF WATER!

It's like Groundhog's Day. It doesn't matter if that fat rodent sees his shadow or not. Spring usually begins on March 20th. Six more weeks of winter and six more weeks until spring are still six weeks! It's all the same. Why do we allow ourselves to be manipulated by some *rat* that could care less about his shadow? He always looks like we've interrupted his nap. And worse, we woke him up for no reason.

Why am I telling you this? Because personality doesn't predict results!

THE MYTH: People assume negative thinking will drag you down into a quagmire of self-loathing and destructive behavior.

THE REALITY: Negative thinking is not *fatalistic* thinking.

Negative thinking means identifying potential problems, things that could go wrong and alternative outcomes other than the one we want. Perfect scenarios rarely happen. Fatalistic thinking is when you think, "no way, no how." It's useless to think it will all fall apart. Negative thinking really means understanding ways things *could* fall apart so you can avoid them *actually* falling apart.

{ What about positive thinking?

They say that, with a positive attitude, you can do anything. Is that true? I mean, is it really true?

I know that, no matter how hard I work and no matter how positive I am, I can never be Miss America. It's a fact. It's never going to happen.

Why?

Well, for one there is an age limit: You need to be between 17 and 24 years old, and those days have long passed me by. For another, I'm married.[8] So I can't be Miss America.

Maybe I can be Mrs. America instead. That would be great. Except for one small problem. Well it's not "small," but enough about me… For those who can't tell by my goatee[9] I am not a woman. So Mrs. America is out, too.

[8] Sorry, ladies. I know how disappointed you must be.

[9] It's a family thing, I have one, my father has one, my grandmother had one.

Maybe Mr. America will work.

I know what you're thinking: "Craig, you delicious piece of man candy, of course you can be Mr. America."

While I appreciate that, let's be realistic.

For me to enter a nationwide beauty contest ... well, things would not end well. Let me put it this way: I don't scare small children and I don't need meat around my neck to play with dogs, but I am under no illusion that I have beauty pageant looks.[10]

I have to look at the reasons for my goal. Understanding why we want a goal can allow us to find other ways of reaching it. This is where negative thinking comes in. Why would I want to be Miss America? I can only think of three reasons:

Reason #1:

I want scholarship money. The Miss America program is a great way for young women to get scholarships for college. Do I need to be Miss America to go to school? Not at all. There are a lot of more effective ways to earn money. There are other scholarships, grants and loans available. God forbid that I have to go work to earn the money and then go back to school a few years down the road.

Reason #2:

I have a social agenda to promote. You have to have a platform to be Miss America—some sort of agenda you wish to enlighten people

---

[10] Though I do admit, I have the legs of Anne Margaret. Anne Margaret on severe hormone therapy, but sexy nonetheless.

on—be it poverty, homelessness, illnesses, injustice … something of significance that could be your cause. Do you need to be Miss America to do that? Not at all. Sure, being a minor celebrity and all might help as far as publicity goes. In the long run, hard work and drive will be more helpful than publicity. You can donate your time, give your money, or start a foundation. Again, you don't need to be Miss America.

Reason #3:

The only other reason I can think of to be Miss America is that you want people to think you're pretty. You don't need to be Miss America to do that. Hang out with ugly people; they'll make you look a lot better. Like the old saying goes, "How can you look thin? Get fat friends." Go find yourself some troglodyte[11] buddies so you'll be the best-looking person in the bunch!

A positive attitude won't always get you everything you want. Keep in mind that I didn't say it's not helpful. I'm simply saying that positivity isn't the end-all and be-all to success that some would have you believe. In fact, we're told to eliminate negativity entirely from our lives. Why would you eliminate a tool from your arsenal?

It's like saying, "Here, build a house, but you can't use a tape measure."

Can you build a house without a tape measure? Sure. Would you want to? Not unless you don't mind living in a crazy, unstable, circus funhouse.

Negativity is just another tool. Why wouldn't you use all the tools you have?

---

[11] troglodyte: The book's first word over the 8th grade reading level!

{ Find the value

Everything has value.

Everything.

If you have fears, worries and doubts, it's your brain telling you "Hey! This could be trouble!" Take a look at why you have those fears or worries. Understanding the cause can often neutralize them.

Fear is not always a bad thing. Fear tells you to run out of a burning building. Fear tells you to put on your seat belt. Fear tells you to double check your work. Being cautious and avoiding problems before they happen is a good thing.

You need a few negative thoughts to keep yourself balanced, protected and prepared so if things don't go as planned, you're not blindsided. Jumping into a situation without a backup plan can be catastrophic, just as getting bogged down with too many horrible scenarios is also ineffective. A positive attitude combined with some negative thinking can lead to success.

Every thought you have has some value to it. There is a reason it exists. Each fear or doubt you have is your brain's way of protecting you from harm.

Is every fear valid? No. Can it be blown out of proportion by our own experiences, attitudes and beliefs? Absolutely. Nevertheless, the fear or doubt is generated to protect you, be it from physical or emotional pain.

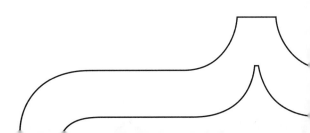

Since the dawn of man our brains have used our negative thoughts for a purpose. Our ancestors' more basic instincts, basic skills and innate abilities skewed toward the negative to save their lives. We still have these instincts.

Why do deer and squirrels immediately run away when they hear any noise? They've been conditioned for generations to run or they will die.

Why does our heart rate increase when we're nervous? The flop sweat and flush feeling that comes out of nowhere? That's our body prepping itself to run. The heart accelerates to get more oxygen throughout the body so we can use that to escape. The fight or flight response kicks in.

Animals eliminate any waste not only to lighten their load (so to speak) but also to leave an overwhelming scent to distract the predator while they run away. It's why some people wet themselves when they get scared. It is instinct from a time long ago.[12]

{ Snakes and spiders

How many people do you know with an irrational fear of spiders? Or snakes? Even Indiana Jones hated snakes! Research shows that humans have evolved to fear snakes and spiders even if the person has never seen one in person.

In one particular study,[13] subjects were able to identify snakes and spiders faster than less dangerous animals like frogs or caterpillars.

[12] It could also just be a weak bladder.

[13] Vanessa LoBue, J. S. (2008, March 3). Detecting the Snake in the Grass: Attention to Fear-Relevant Stimuli by Adults and Young Children. Psychological Science , 284-289.

It's quite logical if you take a moment to think about it.

What common creatures could cause the most trouble, the most often, for humans living, hunting or just plain walking in the forests and jungles? Snakes and spiders.

Our innate fear protects us.

Our fears and doubts exist for a reason. While some may not be as relevant as it was when we roamed the plains, hunting woolly mammoths, they still exist. With a thoughtful, analytical approach you can use these basic instincts to your advantage. Harness them to show you what to avoid in life to make the process easier or to avoid outright catastrophe. Notice I didn't say failure. Failure is not all bad.

No one likes to be afraid. Think of fear as our brain's wake-up call. Our internal Homeland Security.

{ Natural negativity

Our brains naturally lean toward the negative. Scientists say that 75-80 percent of all our thoughts are negative.[14]

What are you thinking right now?

"I am not negative. Nope. Not me. I can't believe this twit thinks I'm negative. How dare him! I am NOT negative. No way! I never have been negative, I never will be negative. Stupid poopyhead!"

Of course, that was several negative statements in row. Don't worry;

[14] Marano, H. E. (2003). Our Brain's Negative Bias. Psychology Today .

I won't take the *poopyhead* comment personally.

This negative bias influences everything that happens to us. How we understand people and how they respond to us.

Take this example:

Jeff is my employee. As part of company policy, every six months I conduct an employee review with Jeff. By leaps and bounds, Jeff is the best employee I have.

During the review I tell him, "If only I had ten more just like you, this place would be gangbusters! You work hard, stay late, and complete every project well above expectations. It wouldn't hurt you to come in on time, but being ten or fifteen minutes late is nothing compared to all the fantastic work that you do. Great job!"

NOW OF THE FOUR THINGS I TOLD HIM:

1. He works hard.

2. He stays late.

3. He completes every project.

4. He comes in late.

Which one is he going to remember?

"My boss thinks I'm a screw-up because I'm late every day."

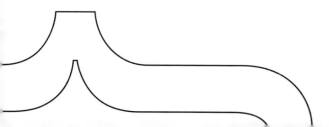

With our brain's natural negativity bias, we have a tendency to be drawn to the negative. We react to and remember negative thoughts and emotions. We can talk all we want about how fabulous someone is, yet if we say one negative to them, usually that's the one comment they take home and chew on.

We could say some of the greatest compliments, yet if we let one minor (to us, anyway) criticism slip out, it could ruin the whole encounter. We need to remember that when we talk to our employees, co-workers, bosses, spouses and children.

I am putting this out there so you'll know:

When we do let a negative come out of our mouths, we need to recognize the power it has. I've heard it takes eleven positive statements to overcome one negative statement. That's a lot of smoke we'll need to puff up someone's rear end for a simple slip of the tongue that really doesn't even matter to us or we may not even believe 100%.

Don't think I'm saying we shouldn't say something negative if it's warranted. Sometimes a well-placed negative statement is the most appropriate thing we can say. A well-delivered negative statement can make people aware of a problem. After all, we can't fix a problem if we don't know it exists.

OBLIGATORY OBSCURE
PHILOSOPHER'S QUOTE:

"If you realized how powerful your thoughts are, you would never think a negative thought."

PEACE PILGRIM

Our thoughts have power? You bet. Some can't warm toast, others burn like supernovas. They all have a purpose.

Peace Pilgrim[15] has a point…but it only goes so far. Negative *thoughts* have the power to protect, prevent and perform. Negative *words* have the power to warn, inform and enlighten.

We can start to see the power of negative thoughts and words. If they have so much power, why do we refuse to utilize them?

{ Resistance is fertile

The opposition to true negative thinking has been under attack now more than ever. Parents, only wanting the best for their children, shelter them from any negative experiences or feelings. It really comes from a generational issue and has been evolving into something more absurd each passing year.

In the 1960's and 70's, as more parents became two income houses, children were left to their own devices. Latchkey kids, a term to describe millions of kids who walked home to an empty house after school, became more and more common. With both parents working, their parent's busy schedules didn't allow for them to go to every school event or be there to cook dinners or help with schoolwork.

As these children grew up into adults, they vowed they would be different parents than their own. They made themselves more available to their children. Is this a bad thing? Of course not! Spending time

---

[15] Sounds like something a Bizzaro John Wayne would say.

with your children is valuable. Teaching them right from wrong, explaining the world to them, and protecting them from the ills of the world. Therein lays the problem.

A new kind of parent has emerged, known as: Helicopter Parents. Helicopter parents wait until there is trouble, swoop in, fix their kids' problems and fly off again waiting for the next situation to occur.

This is the exact opposite of the corporate world's "seagull management," which is where the manager lingers overhead, out of the way, then suddenly swoops in, craps on everybody and flies off.

Helicopter parents also deflect any kind of criticism (constructive or otherwise) away from their offspring, protecting their children's self-esteem and instilling "positive" attitudes. The unintended consequences also created narcissistic children with more self-esteem than sense.

We've hidden them from negative thinking, teaching them that it is an evil, awful thing. Yet if it's a natural part of our thinking, what does that make us?

{ IT'S IN A BOOK SO IT MUST BE TRUE!!!

Did the parents just suddenly decide to be only positive? There wasn't any outside influence on them?

Oh yes…the self-help book.

You probably found this very book in the exact same section as a lot of this metaphysical, touchy feely, marketing machine, over the top crap.

The ones that tell us that we can be a one minute manager by only working four hours a week![16] Or that we can learn the "secret" to being successful.[17] How about the seven steps to being successful?[18] Who cut the cheese?[19]

Many self-help books do offer some great ideas and are immensely useful. Those are not necessarily the ones everyone buys, however. People buy what will make them feel better, not necessarily what will help them. It's like comfort food; though it may make us feel good, it isn't very good for our health. When the empty *get-rich-quick, express train to spirituality*, i.e. *easy* books come out, they get a lot of publicity. Maybe they get on Oprah. If everyone is reading it, it must be good. On that note, *Paul Blart, Mall Cop* was the #1 movie in the country for two straight weeks! It's no Oscar winner by any stretch of the imagination.

Popularity makes people think: *It must be true, it must be good.* If all these *books* tell everyone that negative thinking is bad, it must be.

Negative thinking *isn't* bad. Positive thinking is just more magical sounding, and easier for people to believe. The more the same old things get repeated, the more we all believe in things.[20]

---

[16] Sure, if you already have hundreds of thousands of dollars to outsource everything!

[17] Here's a clue: stop wishing, get off your ass, and get working!

[18] Oh wait, you need to buy my other book on step 8! And the next book on step 9.

[19] That is the title, isn't it?

[20] For the record: Mikey of LIFE cereal fame did not die from mixing POP Rocks and Pepsi.

OBLIGATORY

FAMOUS GURU QUOTE:

"The current perception I get from the evening news is that the world is dominated by human failure, crime, catastrophe, corruption, and tragedy. We are all tuning in to see how the human mind is evolving, but the media keeps hammering home the opposite, that the human mind is mired in darkness and folly."

DEEPAK CHOPRA

{ Blame the media

What really gives negativity a bad rap is the media.

We all know bad news sells newspapers. "If it bleeds it leads."

Let me ask you this. Would *you* be more likely to pick up a paper that read "Everything's Fine!" or one that said: "Headless Body Found in Topless Bar"?[21]

---

[21] I wish that was a joke, but it appeared in the New York Post in 1982.

Now that kind of stuff sells newspapers!

Local TV is even worse. During sweeps, we see commercials like: "There's something in your house that can kill your children! Tomorrow at 11."

Tomorrow? Tomorrow? Why can't you tell me right now? I hope my kids live long enough for me to see this!

THEY DO THAT TO DRAW OUR ATTENTION TO THEM.

1. It's vague: "There's something."

2. It's personal: "in your house."

3. It's dangerous: "that can kill." It hits at something you hold dearest: "your children."

It's almost always some rare, less than 1% chance kind of situation. For example: "If you're remodeling your home and you leave out exposed wires, your children can grab hold of those wires, stick them in their mouths and electrocute themselves!"

Look, if you're letting your children roam around a work site with live, bare electrical wires... Child Services will be there shortly. Please don't put up a fuss. It's really for the best.

The weather is the worst. They always make the weather more negative than it needs to be. It's not the Weather Center; it's the Severe Weather Center.

It's not Sunshine Central, it's Storm Central.

They also like to scare us and make it sound worse than it is. When Hurricane Rita came, local news stations in Houston, Texas were on twenty-four hours a day for three days in advance. They created animations showing how the potential flood surge would wipe out the entire east side of Houston as well as Galveston.

We could *see* how excited the weathermen were just talking about the devastation it might cause. As the hurricane slowly turned away, we could also see the disappointment in their faces.

"It's...it's not coming. In fact, it's heading to the Sabine River area, one of the...least...populated areas. So it looks like this is the (gulp) best case scenario."

I spoke to a meteorologist after Hurricane Rita and he said, "You have to forgive us. Hurricanes are like our Super Bowl."

I've seen the Super Bowl. At the end of the game, they don't kill all the spectators and blow up the stadium.

Remember in the old days, if a storm got close to Cuba they would tell us about it. Now, if a pygmy burps off the coast of Africa, we're watching clouds for three weeks.

One time, I was watching a baseball game and the weather alert came scrawling across the bottom. "Hurricane Ernesto....1900 miles from Houston." 1900 miles!! My parents live in Concord, NH. It's roughly 1800 miles from Houston. At that moment, they were more a direct threat to me than the hurricane!

If the weather isn't bad enough, they make it worse. They invent things like heat indexes and wind chills.

"It'll be 98 degrees today, but the heat index will be 104!"

"Today's low is 13 degrees but the wind chill will be -30!"

Like 13 degrees isn't bad enough, they have to make it sound like we live in Antarctica. You may even freeze to the sidewalk!

I understand the importance of knowing the weather and being pre-pared. Do they need to scare people into watching, when they would do a greater service by simply telling them the information?

This leads to the "Crying Wolf" Syndrome. All these scare tactics slowly desensitize the viewers, trust erodes and then when a real emergency happens, no one believes them. The same can happen to us if all we ever do is tell everyone how awful it will always be.[22]

I will be the first to say that even though I talk about negativity and how it can be useful, in the wrong hands and in the wrong amounts it can be dangerous. Not unlike gasoline. Sadly, the news likes to use gasoline to light fires under their viewers.

Every couple of years, the news will overwhelm us with "Shark At-tack" headlines. Stories on bites, attacks and the occasional deaths. Remember the "Summer of the Shark" in 2001?

During the "Summer of the Shark," all of the news channels were blasting tales of people in danger from sharks. They neglected to tell us that attacks were actually down 15% that year but since an eight-year old boy was bitten and lost his arm, it made the news, twenty-four hours a day for weeks.

---

[22] This is fatalistic thinking. Not negative thinking.

Do you know how many people on average are attacked by sharks in the United States each year? Less than thirty-seven. And killed by a shark? Less than one. From 1990 to 2006, twelve people were killed by shark attacks.[23]

Do you know how many people died from sand collapsing on them while digging at the beach? Sixteen. That means it's statistically safer in the water than on the shore![24]

Informing people is useful. Scaring people isn't.

We've got to look at the reality of negative thinking, pull it out of its hole in the ground, and look at its shadow so we can get a real understanding of its usefulness.

And let sleeping groundhogs lie.

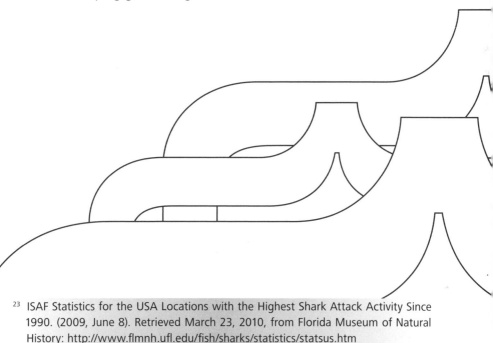

[23] ISAF Statistics for the USA Locations with the Highest Shark Attack Activity Since 1990. (2009, June 8). Retrieved March 23, 2010, from Florida Museum of Natural History: http://www.flmnh.ufl.edu/fish/sharks/statistics/statsus.htm

[24] B. A. Maron, T. S. Haas, and B. J. Maron (21 Jun, 2007) Sudden Death from Collapsing Sand Holes , New England Journal of Medicine

CHAPTER 1:

The Audacity of "Nope"

"NO" IS AN IMPORTANT WORD AND IT IS OKAY TO SAY. HOWEVER, FOR A LOT OF PEOPLE, "NO" IS A VERY HARD WORD TO SAY. WE GREW UP THINKING "NO" IS A BAD THING AND HAVE BEEN CONDITIONED NOT TO SAY "NO."

Think about it. When you were growing up, what did you hear the most? "No."

"Can I have this?" *"No."*

"Can I eat that?" *"No."*

"Can I burn this?" *"NO!"*

"No" was never a happy word. Then, as we got older, as we learned to walk and talk, we decided we'll try this "no" thing out.

"Clean your room."

"No."

How did that work out? Probably not very well. We learned that nothing good ever comes from "no."

{ **THE MYTH:** Saying "no" is defying authority. It makes us look unsupportive or possibly combative.

{ **THE REALITY:** Saying "no" is an important way to manage our time, help people make proper choices and get control over our lives.

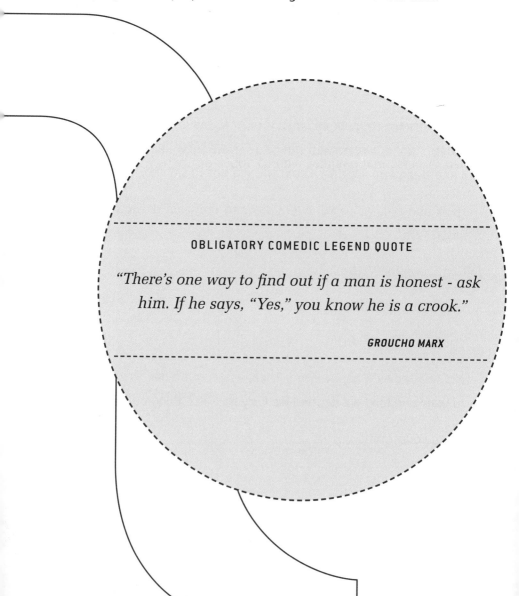

OBLIGATORY COMEDIC LEGEND QUOTE

"There's one way to find out if a man is honest - ask him. If he says, "Yes," you know he is a crook."

GROUCHO MARX

{ First, kill all the "yes" men

Many of us have a hard time taking constructive criticism.[25] People see any form of criticism or any opposition to an idea they have as a personal affront. If they don't like my idea, they must not like me, they don't respect me, or I've done something wrong.

This causes people to get irritated. We need to learn how to take criticism properly. Seems like more and more people are surrounding themselves only with "yes" men. Sure it's good to hear it, but we don't learn anything that way, other than this person thinks we're great. It doesn't help us find the answers we need.

One of the worst things we can do is surround ourselves with "yes" men. A person who agrees with us 100% of the time is 100% useless. Sad but true. If you're looking for a way to cut back or streamline the office, find that one person who always says "You are great!" or "That's an ingenious idea!" all the time. That's the one you get rid of.

I don't need someone telling me how great I am all the time. I'm well aware of that fact. I don't need to hear someone tell me how great my idea is. It's my idea! Of course it's great. What I do need is someone saying, "Hold on a second. That idea's pretty good…I see a potential problem." Or "That's fine. What about another option?"

It's always good to have at least one person in our group with a negative mindset. At least one, but no more than two. More than two and we'll want to shoot ourselves. Try to include a person who doesn't always agree with you. Having a dissenting voice allows us to

---

[25] Try not to take that statement the wrong way. Wow, you are touchy!

see other sides of a situation. Even if they are wrong 99% of the time, they often will highlight areas where our idea may have problems.

I once heard a CEO, after a board meeting, explain the value of a negative opinion. Upon every idea that was proposed during the meeting, this one board member always had a complaint, pointing out a flaw, and was just downright cranky.

Someone asked the CEO, "Why do you keep him around? He's so negative."

The CEO replied, "He shows me what needs to be fixed."

By not letting the delivery system interfere with the message, the CEO was able to use the negativity for positive results.

Abraham Lincoln was perfect at avoiding the "yes" man. When you hear this concept of "Team of Rivals," this was attributed to Lincoln. When he became president he appointed people who either didn't like him, was an enemy from the other party, or they thought he was a big, tall, lanky redneck who was only good for a joke or idle conversation. The reason he put these people on his cabinet was the fact that they were the best person for that particular job. For Treasury he selected Salmon Chase, who did a magnificent job. He did it so well so he could spend all of his free time trying to undermine Lincoln in hopes he could win the presidential nomination when Lincoln's first term was over. Lincoln had plenty of opportunities to get rid of Chase and he was well aware of the back office politics going on. He didn't. For the simple fact that Chase was too valuable at Treasury and the country needed him there. Oh, after Chase got the US back on solid financial footing and still tried to sneak behind Lincoln, the president got rid of him. Yet, he still supported Chase's appointment to the

Supreme Court. Again, because he knew that he would be the best for that position as well.

He chose these people not because it was good for Abraham Lincoln and not because it was good for the Republican Party; he chose them because it was good for the country. When we make educated decisions, and the key word is educated, we need to gather as much information as possible. A hunch or a gut feeling is usually the subconscious mind telling us something we already know to be true. When it comes to things we don't know about, a hunch could turn a bad idea into a major mistake. We can have all the bad ideas we want. You know why? They are just thoughts. Ideas go as fast as they arrive in our head. Mistakes are things we have to overcome. Actions are things we cannot take back.

"Yes" men are dangerous. They can allow flawed ideas to live and grow into major mistakes. "Yes" men don't think, don't adapt and certainly don't move an organization forward. We need to get all perspectives.

{ The myth of "should"

I like to think human beings, at their very core, want to help others. We all want to say "yes" and be a resource for people. This, however, can lead to the mentality of 'I should'. This mentality needs to be drastically reduced.

I hear all the time, people complaining how they "should" be able to do something.

"I should be able to find the time…"

"I should be more helpful…"

"I should be able to have a career and have a family and have a social life, etc."

They want it all, not knowing how much time, effort and work go into having "it all." They see other people, people they know, co-workers, or outright strangers living their lives and wonder "Why can't I be like them? I should be able to."

We see others out there and think we "should" be like them.

"If Oprah Winfrey and Martha Stewart can do it, so can I!"

Yet, if we look at Oprah and Martha, we can start to understand that what they are doing and how it is getting done is far too much for one person.

Oprah is an inspirational story of a small town girl who worked her way up the TV ranks to get a national syndicated show that she uses to help women and children across the globe. She builds schools in impoverished nations, gives gifts to those in need and highlights the issues that often go overlooked in society. Doing all that good, many women strive to follow in her footsteps. Only they forget that Oprah is the figurehead and she has a staff of several hundred working behind the scenes to get Oprah's vision to come to fruition. Even Oprah can't do what Oprah is doing without massive amounts of help.

Martha Stewart is another story. Many women look up to her as the ideal when it comes to how we should entertain, host a party, keep a home and live our lives. Honestly, is she any better than anyone else?

She's got a prison record. Do you? If you don't, as far as I'm concerned, you're doing better than she is.

Of course, being celebrities, they work very hard to make sure we are only seeing what they allow us to see.

You're at Starbucks and you see a mother and her three angelic kids. They're saying "please" and "thank you", behaving properly. Maybe you think to yourself, "Why can't my kids behave like that? I should have kids who behave, too." You have seen a sliver, an unbelievable tiny fraction of this person's life. Like a lot of snapshots, it looks pretty good, but you have no idea what that person's life is like. Maybe she was screaming and yelling, threatening the kids in the car before they went into the coffee shop. It could be sheer coincidence that the children are behaving in that moment, because the rest of the time they're bloody monsters! My point is, you don't know. You can only go by what you see in that moment. Yet, you compare that moment to your entire life. Is that fair? When you're out in the world, you only get a snapshot of a person's life. Maybe in that snapshot, everything looks ideal.

Even society's past culture influences the perception of what we "should" be doing in the present.

We certainly haven't leveled the responsibilities between men and women yet. We put far too much of life's daily burdens on them. The men reading this book won't like this but I have to tell the truth. When women delegate responsibility to men, we screw them up on purpose. We do it on purpose so we don't have to do it again. Which is why we don't just screw up; we screw up in such a spectacular fashion to make sure our wives don't give us anything to work on.

Mothers, I feel, get the raw end of the 'should' stick. They go to work, they come home, a lot of them not only clean up after their kids, and they clean up for another bigger kid.[26] Basically, what I am saying is, if you are a married woman with two children, you really have three children.

There's the myth that women "should" be doing all the housework. Well, I'm telling you to put a stop to that right now. Get him to do some housework! He works too, I understand that. You both work, so you both "should" do the housework. Let him do some laundry. Give him a stunt load first. Don't just give him reds and whites on the first try. Not unless you like everything pink. I would suggest starting off with towels, that way if he ruins those, you still have some nice rags. Never, ever let him touch the delicates.

One time, I was trying to be the good husband. I honestly wasn't trying to screw things up, but to all the men reading this: never wash a bra. I have no idea what they're made of.[27] I put it in the dryer and it came out a twisted mess of torn cloth and mangled wire poking out everywhere. It looked like a satellite exploded. My wife looked at it and said, "You expect me to wear that?"

"It lifts and separates."

"Yeah. It lifts and separates my skin from my body!"

Make him do some chores around the house. Split them up. My wife and I split our bills in half. I pay certain bills, she pays other bills. That way we're both responsible for paying bills. If one is better at paying

[26] A.k.a. the Husband

[27] I think mostly steel beams and kryptonite.

bills than the other, shift duties around so both have equal responsibility. Just don't load up one person over the other.

You "should" be able to do what you "can" do. Pretty simplistic statement, yet true, nonetheless. If you can't be at every soccer game, every dance recital, every school play, then you can't. That's the truth. If you can't make it, then you shouldn't make it. People get caught up in the ideal life and let's face it: the ideal life doesn't exist. People think they deserve it all and maybe they do[28] but actually getting it all, very unlikely.

I try to get as much out of life as I can, but I know I can't get it all. If you want more time with your family, you need to make that time up somewhere else. Maybe you take it from work or your social calendar. You want more social time, so you say, "Sorry family, can't spend as much time with you as I used to. Work needs me, so I don't have as much social time to spend with you."

It's the "grass is always greener" syndrome.

Stop trying to compete.

It really is that simple.

OBLIGATORY OBSCURE HUMORIST QUOTE

"Half of the troubles of this life can be traced to saying 'yes' too quickly and not saying 'no' soon enough."

JOSH BILLINGS

[28] I doubt it, but hey, that's their problem, not mine.

{ Saying "no"

While saying no can be intimidating, we need to identify some things to think about before we commit to a "yes" or "no".

Think about what "yes" means.

Don't say "yes" to something if you can't do it. Think about the amount of time, effort and resources "yes" will entail. If you honestly feel you can do it, you can choose to accept.

At work, if a supervisor hands us an assignment, as irritating as that might be, they expect it to get done. Often, they have more than one person they need to oversee. The more people, the more likely they may not necessarily know what we are working on at any given moment. They come rushing to us with an emergency, forgetting we're already working on an important assignment. If we blindly agree to this new assignment, one of the two things we're working on is not going to get done. We need to turn the decision back onto the supervisor. Ask them "Is this new assignment more important than what I am already working on?" Let them make the decision, isn't that what they get paid the big bucks for?

 They may think we should be able to get both things done. They may also realize we've got a full plate and prioritize for us. We need to allow them to see what we're working on, so they can see what's more important.

Simply put, a manager wants to make sure the work gets done. They don't necessarily care who does it. If we can't do it, they want to know. They want to know so they can take it to someone who can get it done. They forget they just doubled our workload, that the only reason they came to us in the first place is that we're their best employee. If we take the assignment and we don't finish it, suddenly, in their eyes, we look undependable. Maybe they don't trust us with big assignments anymore.

Managers would much rather hear we can't get something done than to have us say yes and when the deadline approaches, find out we can't get it done. Not only are we screwed for not finishing the job, they're screwed because they delegated it to us. If we let that happen, we become, in their eyes, someone who is undependable and untrustworthy. The only thing in life we truly own and control is our integrity. It's important that we monitor our integrity by making honest judgments about what we can and cannot take on.

Obviously, there are certain instances where we have to take on assignments, where we have to say "yes". This is "work" after all. Not every day can be the perfect scenario. We need to make sure our supervisor knows what we are working on so they can make the best decisions when delegating. If we constantly say "yes" to everything, then can't deliver, we start looking bad. Which is what we were trying to avoid by saying "yes" to everything!

Ever have a friend ask you for help in a passive aggressive way? They casually forget to tell you exactly how much help they really need, because they're afraid of hearing "no".

They start out innocently enough.

"I just have this dresser; it's too big for just me. It'll only take twenty minutes."

Yeah, right.

As soon as you step foot into their apartment, house, or condo they've got you in their spider trap. Guess what? You're not going to just help move a dresser. You know if someone asks for help moving, it never takes only twenty minutes and they've got more than one heavy thing in the house. They've got couches, boxes, furniture, pool tables; all kinds of big, clunky crap for you to haul. You thought saying "no" was hard before! It's really difficult to say "no", at *their* house, while you're holding a box of *their* stuff you've already moved.

You don't need to answer at that moment.

Ask if you can think about it. This way you can take the time you need to think about what "yes" means. If they need an answer that second, say "no".[29] If they can't give you the common courtesy of thinking it over, you can give a guilt free "no" every time. If they ask for an answer right then and there, kindly explain that you are in the middle of something at this moment and don't want to commit to something you may not be able to do.

Often they try and trick you into admitting you have an open calendar with innocent questions like, "What are you up to this weekend?" This is the first step in laying the trap. They're setting you up to lock you into their schedule by getting you to tell them yours is free. If you answer with any sort of timetable, they will find ways to work around

---

[29] Unless the question is "Do you want a million dollars, no strings attached?" "Yes please!"

it. If you say "Oh nothing." Guess what? You've got something now.

A good response is to answer their question with a more direct question like my standby response:

"Why, what's going on?"

Now they have to tell you what their devious plan is without you exposing your leisure time! Once they tell you, you can make up your own mind on your terms.

Make sure "No" means "No."

Don't be wishy-washy. If you don't say anything other than "no", all they will hear is "Yes!" You've left the door open. If you leave an inch open, they will try their hardest to rip that door wide open and get you to commit. I call it the weasel effect. They try to weasel a "yes" out of you as long as you don't actually say "no". Don't be afraid to say "no", especially if it's a valid reason.

For example: If someone asks if you can help them this weekend, avoid terms like:

I'll see if I can.

I'll try.

If I have the time.

Most likely.[30]

---

[30] Regardless if it is a yes or no, the word "likely" doesn't mean anything so to them, you're still available

I don't think I'll be able to.[31]

Perhaps.

If I have the chance.

I doubt it.[32]

It doesn't look good.[33]

Of course, there are times when we have to say "yes". While we have commitments to family, friend and work, we are not slaves to them. We are not indentured servants that have to cater to everyone else's whims.

Pick and choose your "no's".

Did I just say you should pick and chew your nose?! Eww. Sorry, I think I just made myself a little sick.

Anyway, saying "no" too many times will cause problems. There are times, and we've all had them, when "no" is the correct and perfect response.

If you can lose your fear of "no", you'll be happier and more productive.

I probably "should" have written a better chapter (other authors write so much better, so much clearer)…but this is as good as I "can" do.

---

[31] Again, thinking is suspect. People think Bigfoot exists, UFOs abduct people solely to do anal probes and Jessica Simpson is talented. Exactly how trustworthy is their thinking?

[32] Doubt is still something that can be changed.

[33] Still means it could improve. Or you're a Magic 8-Ball.

[Realist's Guidelines]
The Audacity of "Nope"

* Saying "no" is an important way to manage your time, help people make proper choices and get control over your life.

* A person who agrees with you 100% of the time is 100% useless.

* A hunch or a gut feeling is usually the subconscious mind telling you something you already know to be true.

* Reality Check: Martha Stewart is an ex-con.[34]

* For the husbands: If you've never washed one before, never wash a bra without supervision!

* You "should" be able to do what you "can" do

* Before we commit to a yes or no:
  * Think about what "yes" means
  * You don't need to answer immediately. If so, answer "no".

* "No" means "no"!

---

[34] Just makes me feel good knowing she's not really better than me.

FOR THE POSITIVE THINKERS:

Maybe "no" isn't for you. Just like saying "no" is a choice, saying "yes' is too. Feel free to take on as much as you'd like. Say "yes" to everything. "Yes" opens doors, makes people happy, allows you to have new experiences, new ideas, new lifestyles. Who knows? The world could very well be one "Yes" away!

CHAPTER 2:

Hope for the Best, Plan for the Worst

OLD BEN FRANKLIN HAD IT RIGHT.[35] GOOD OLD BENJAMIN UNDERSTOOD THAT HOPE ALONE IS NOT ENOUGH.

Hope without action, without planning, without work is just wishing. Hope is only necessary when the tools to achieve are not currently available.

People hope for greater things than they have or think are possible to attain or achieve.

---

[35] No, not his preoccupation with French prostitutes.

People hope for something when they cannot honestly know the result.

Without hope, we have no drive; we have no desire.

Why do anything unless there is the hope things will improve? If not for yourself, someone else.

Hope is great. If hope is all you have, you, my *hopeful* friend, are in some serious trouble. Because unbridled hope that nothing will or can go wrong is a fool's illusion.

If all you do is hope for something, then you are ill-prepared for any other outcome.

Often ignoring a negative outcome causes much worse problems. Hope is often a replacement for action: If we can just *hope* it happens, in our minds we're *doing* something, though in reality you are doing *nothing*. Without thinking ahead of what could go wrong we end up walking headlong into a buzz saw of problems we could have easily avoided.

OBLIGATORY FOUNDING FATHER QUOTE – PART DEUX:

"By failing to prepare you are preparing to fail."

BEN FRANKLIN

{ Strength from weakne

We're all taught that we should be strong, even though we... We're taught to be fearless, even though we all have fears.

Any hint of weakness is to be camouflaged. The sheer thought that there *may* be a potential problem is considered a weakness.

We are taught to tell everyone how well we are doing, how good business is, how smart and wonderful our families are. No one wants to hear about how horrible your life is.

I learned early not to ask my grandmother, "How are you?" because she would tell me! Often, in long, drawn out, graphical detail about her latest ailment. Believe me when I tell you that the scars from her stories of gastrointestinal issues[36] still haven't healed.

Do we need to run from our weaknesses? Should we keep them hidden away like mental booby traps, only to deal with them once we've done something that set them off and now we're neck deep in trouble?

Without an honest assessment of who we are, both what works and what we're deficient with, how can we possibly achieve the greatness we've been telling everyone?

Look at this quote from the coach[37] of an NFL football team:

"There's a lot of things that we didn't do as well as we needed to do as a football team. You name it, it was a problem. We gave up

---

[36] I can't look at feta cheese to this day!

[37] Spoiler alert! The coach's name is Bill Belichick

a couple long turns. Defensively, there were signs we didn't play well. Offensively, we didn't play well, but when we did play well it was in the fourth quarter, when we needed to make those plays, and that was important. The coaching plan, certainly, needed a lot of improvement."

The same team's quarterback:[38]

"We have to execute better, run better routes, throw better passes, make better catches, block better."

And the same team's safety:[39]

"I felt that this was the first time all year that we got bullied. We can't allow teams to run the ball and pound it like that. There are times this is a *Mano-a-Mano* battle and they were winning it. Tonight's game showed we have a lot of problems and we're going to look at film and make corrections..."

Sounds pretty dire, huh? Not really. They won that game. That team's record at the time? 12-0.

See, the 2007 New England Patriots didn't look at their success and rest on their laurels. They were constantly trying to improve, analyzing what went wrong, even when they won.

They never settled for being good when the goal was to be great. They strived to play the perfect game and were never satisfied with anything less.

---

[38] Spoiler alert! The player's name is Tom Brady

[39] Spoiler alert! the safety's name is Rodney Harrison. Isn't learning athlete's names fun?

DON'T BE AFRAID TO ASK YOURSELF THE FOLLOWING QUESTIONS:

1. Are you set up to be undefeated?

2. If not, what are some things that might cost you a victory down the road?

3. What am I doing with my life/company/relationship that I need to correct?

4. Where am I lacking? Am I missing certain skills that would take me farther than I am today?

5. What is the one thing you can't afford to lose?

Why is this guy asking me so many damn questions? I already bought the book. This is too much of a commitment for me. Can't we just be friends? I think we need some time apart.[40]

THE MYTH: You have to only focus on your strengths. Any acknowledgment of your weakness will ultimately make you feel weak.

THE REALITY: Your innate strengths can only take you so far. To reach your potential you need to identify weaknesses and find solutions to them.

Both you and I aren't always perfect. My wife will attest I am far from it. As will my parents, my teachers, my co-workers and possibly even you, if pressed for an answer. At least I will always try to be a better

[40] Feel free to put the book down for a bit. If you're still at the bookstore, buy the book and read it later. Or not at all. Just be sure to buy the book.

person, have a better life, and be a better friend while knowing that perfection is unattainable.

Constantly attempting to be perfect can be a tough way to live your life. You can be *happy* without being *satisfied.* Honestly, you never will be satisfied.

Your brain always wants to do something. When you achieve a goal, it just comes up with another one. Why do you think so many retired people take up golf? It's a game that you can never master. It constantly challenges you. If you do well one day, you may suck horribly the next. Even Tiger Woods still has bad rounds from time to time.[41] Michael Jordan didn't hit every shot he took.

This inability to be sated has helped the human species improve. Without it, we'd still be just fat monkeys in a tree looking around going, "This is the life!" Well, we wouldn't be saying that since we wouldn't have evolved enough for language, but you get the idea.

We're always trying to improve. You can only get better by taking an honest look at the missteps you're taking.

Don't be afraid to identify *what went wrong.*

Know your strengths. Keep them honed. Then put them in your back pocket, confident that you have them with you at all times.

At some point you will max out your strengths and will be unable to improve. We all reach the ceiling for any individual skill or attribute. To move forward, you need to know your weaknesses. Find ways to overcome them.

[41] Thanksgiving of 2009 jumps to mind.

Write down your strengths. Feel free to write in the book. It feels kinds liberating doesn't it?

My strengths are:

_____

_____

_____

_____

If you don't have any, write down "Good Judgment", since you're reading this you must have some good judgment somewhere. The poor judgment people put this book down a chapter ago.

Now write down what you need to keep those strengths strong. Think of it as exercise for your skills. Like any muscle, strengths can weaken without use. They can be simple things like playing Sudoku[42] to keep your mind sharp. If you're an organized person, making lists or whatever system you have may be your exercise that keeps you super organized.

I keep strong by:

_____

_____

_____

[42] A game I am horrible at. I call it Does-Suck-oh!

Now we're going to do something that we've been told the sheer act of examining is a weakness.

My weaknesses are:

_____

_____

_____

_____

What do you do to get by? Outsource? Hire a person with the skills you lack? Classes? Cheat off the person next to you?

The good thing is that you don't always need to be the person who has to overcome your own weaknesses. You can't possibly do everything and let's be honest, you can't do everything well. We all have our unique talents that we excel at. We also do a lot of things very badly. Write how you think you can compensate for your weaknesses. Hoping they improve is not an option!

I can compensate by:

_____

_____

_____

_____

OBLIGATORY PROVERB:

"A chain is only as strong as its weakest link."

Take your average salesperson, for example. Salespeople are notoriously bad at paperwork.

Sniffing out leads, making contacts, closing deals, that's their bread and butter. Once the deal closes, the long arduous task of filling out order forms and contracts just doesn't give them the rush of selling.

Go to any sales team. Find the person with the highest sales, they are usually the worst at completing paperwork.

Do you fire that person? Not if they're your best revenue generator. That would be foolish and irresponsible! If they truly make that much money for the company, then it's in the best interest of the company to hire a sales assistant. The overhead accrued is more than offset by the income generated.

If you're not in a position where you can hire an assistant, partner up with someone who can pick up your slack. Ideally, you do something they're not the greatest at and as a team you will be fantastic, far better than if either of you were alone.

A good manager will look at the skill sets available to them and look at where the weaknesses lie. When additional people are needed, you'll hire someone who helps round out the team, so the whole organization improves, not just one aspect of it.

We all have our obvious strengths and underlying weaknesses. Facing our weaknesses and looking at our flaws and inabilities is the only way we can improve, succeed and overcome.

I was once told that focusing on your weaknesses will ultimately make you *feel* weak.

Really? How weak do you feel when you try your hardest and still fail because you refused to admit you couldn't do something? Because you refused to find a way to make up for your own deficiency?

Finding complementary pieces in our work and lives makes us better people. The great thing is the world is full of those missing pieces. You have some pieces someone else is looking for.

We all interconnect; we all fit in the same puzzle. No one person has all the right pieces.

What pieces do you need to be better?

_____

_____

_____

_____

Who has them? Where can you find these missing pieces?

_____

_____

_____

_____

{ Sometimes the worst is sometimes the best

OBLIGATORY FORTUNE COOKIE WISDOM STATEMENT:

"When life hands you lemons, make lemonade!"

Really? Lemonade? Why not just sell lemons?

People need lemons. Every bar in America has lemons. Why not sell them to those dopes that are making way too much lemonade?

Why do people feel they have to always turn something into something else? Why can't they use it for what it is?

Dwelling on negative outcomes can be overwhelming, cause stress and can eat you up from within. Looking at possible negative results is far different then dwelling. It's called dwelling, because like a small building (a dwelling), you can just sit there, immobile from fear and doubt.

The opposite of dwelling, blind faith (or ignorance) can be just as perilous, as we leap from a frying pan of doubt into the proverbial fire of avoidable mistakes. Often, the blind faith that things will work out on their own will get us in trouble.

Blind faith is simply the belief, without any shred of proof, possibly the belief in spite of proof, that forces us to commit to an action.

Often blind faith is the lazy way of just letting events take their course without having to actively participate. We'll just go on faith and if it all works out or crashes and burns, well…it was just meant to be.

Let's take global warming as an example.

I've heard the argument from apathetic people who say, "Oh, they'll figure something out. They'll invent something to take care of this whole situation." Look, my parents are in their 60's. Since they were kids, they've been promised flying cars.

They're still waiting. They probably will live their entire lives without ever seeing the mass production of flying cars. Technology, as cutting edge and amazing as some things are, isn't as fast as we think.

Just think of all the long lines we would avoid at the airport. No more pat downs or stupid rules about packing small bottles of 3.5 oz or less. Why can't my five buddies and I just combine our 3.5oz on the plane for 17.5oz? See, stupid rule.

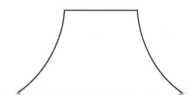

Then again, we're surrounded with people on the road who have a hard enough time driving in two dimensions, never mind adding a third. Just imagine granny flying off into a farmers market. Not a pretty sight. But a promise of a flying car is still a promise, damn it!!

We have cars that park themselves, have built-in maps with little voices that command us to "turn left" even if there isn't a road to turn on to. We can listen to any type of music commercial-free while we drive down the highway. Proof things *do* progress, just not always things that we would like.

Look at your cell phone. If it's anything like mine, they've added cameras, mp3 players, the Internet, you name it. As far as I can tell, my old cell phone from 1997 had the best reception and every phone I've owned since they keep getting worse and worse from a reception standpoint. Why? The technology isn't there, apparently. If it is, it isn't the main feature from a sales perspective. There is no reason for the cell phone industry to improve reception. They can cover up for the lousy service by adding…a crappy camera!

Here's a real clunky analogy[43] for positive vs. negative thinking.

Think of yourself as a car. Sleek, high-performing, super sexy. Me? I'm more like a Plymouth Reliant. Cheap, dependable, low maintenance.

All cars need to do two things. Go and stop.

Positive thinking is the gas pedal. It moves us to our goals. Negative thinking is the brake, slowing us down when we come to potholes or that nasty dead skunk in the road. We need both positive and negative thinking to travel to wherever we're going.

[43] All books are required by law to have them. I'm sure I'll have more coming up but I figured I'd get it out of the way early.

Unfortunately, positive thinking has become a bit twisted in the past hundred years or so.[44]

Positive thinking started with the "New Thought" movement in the mid 1800's. Offered up as a counter to good old fashioned "Calvinism,"[45] it was the feel good hit of the summer.

Calvinism is a somewhat repressive belief that all men are sinners; that no one is *without* sin and quite frankly, *nothing* you do will change that. Calvinists believe that we need to examine all the sins in our lives, regardless of whether we're headed towards heaven or not.[46]

So "New Thought" was put out there. It was just as extreme as Calvinism, only in the *opposite* direction. For people in this new positive-thinking movement, God, spirit and mind all co-existed in happiness.

That meant if you were sick, it must have just been a big mistake, since the entire world that God created was perfect. It was how you *thought* that screwed everything up. In essence, the idea was that you could heal yourself through *thought*, because all disease was created by the mind…

So, lest I confuse you further, my point is back then, either you were sick because *God* wanted you to be (Calvinism), or you *made* yourself sick by thinking the wrong thoughts (New Thought). Sounds dangerous, regardless of which you chose.

---

[44] Here comes the history lesson you knew was coming…

[45] No, class, Calvinism isn't the overwhelming need to pee on the opposition, that's Calvin-and-Hobbes-ism.

[46] Sounds like a blast doesn't it? Makes me want to stay home and go to the church of St. Mattress.

As both movements grew and as "New Thought" progressed, it became more popular, since it gave power back to the *person*.

You could *attract* good things by *thinking* good things; and you would attract *bad* things by *thinking* bad things.

"You must not allow yourself to dwell for a single moment on any kind of negative thought."

EMMET FOX – NEW THOUGHT LEADER

Emmet, you just told people *not* to do something. How very negative. Why couldn't you have said, "You must always focus on *positive* thinking every waking hour..."? Much more positive.

It's no secret; I'm not a big fan of "The Secret."

The whole idea that if you *think* positively about something you want, you will *get* it just doesn't jibe with me.

If you're hoping for a gold necklace, it's not just going to show up. You have to buy it. Or someone else is going to have to give it to you. It's not just going to show up like it does in "The Secret".

Here's the secret to "The Secret": Tell the people they can get anything they want by thinking of it. What could be easier?!

I call "Bullshit."[47]

---

[47] Please excuse the French. And why do we blame the French for all the swearing? Italians do it so much better and with more flair!

Bad things happen to good people every day. That's been one of the biggest mysteries facing organized religion for thousands of years. Why does this happen?

Because bad things *do* happen to good people every day. Not because someone has a bad attitude.

For all the grief I give Oprah, I do know that she is a good person with nothing but the best intentions. When Oprah opened her girl's school in Africa I'm sure she didn't want problems for these children. Yet claims of abuse popped up regardless of Oprah's intentions and daily mantras.

I will grant you that a positive attitude will make the experience of bad things more tolerable, yet it doesn't affect the outcome. If that were true, more people would die on roller coasters, horror movies and airplanes.

Roller coasters are designed to thrill you. Yet many people are terrified while on them. The Law of Attraction states that your roller coaster car should fly off the tracks because you're worried it will.

After seeing *Silence of the Lambs*, I should have been killed by a serial killer. I sure worried about it enough. Yet here I am, typing away.

Every time, and I mean every time, we start landing in an airplane, I start worrying. From the sounds of the muffled cries of fear from the some of the other passengers, I am not alone. How come most of us have never javelined into the tarmac?

If this Law of Attraction is true, what happens if two people with opposing views meet? Whose thoughts win out? Do they explode like matter touching anti-matter?

Do plane crashes happen because everyone thought the plane would crash? Or does the pilot have to outthink the 200 some odd passengers on board with his positive thinking instead of grabbing the controls?

I'll I stop the examples with this:

2004.

Boston Red Sox.

World Champions.

You will never convince me that millions of Red Sox fans were thinking after game 3 of the ALCS vs. The Yankees, "We can do it." They weren't.

We were all depressed and sure it was over. Yet the Red Sox miraculously prevailed. Many, many fans held their breath until the final out of Game 4 of the World Series, waiting for it to all go up in flames. It didn't.

One thing that's missing from the whole Law of Attraction phenomenon is the *action*. Where is the *to-do* part?

Nothing in life is easy. Yet that is the appeal of "The Secret." Believers in "The Secret" are taught that they can just wish their cares away… Not without action you can't! There needs to be a *do* part.

Want that gold necklace? You need to save for it.

Want that promotion? Find out what they are looking for and show them you are the best person for the position.

Want to be a movie star? Get real![48]

Just sitting at home wishing it was so and acting like you already are a movie star won't help. In fact, if you act like a movie star around your friends…they won't be for long. You need to get acting lessons, headshots, demo tapes…

What did I hear you say? This is not as easy as "The Secret"? I know.

Realism is how *successful* people succeed. They *work* for it.

When it comes to the environment,[49] the health of the population, and the survival of a planet…you have to assume the worst.

I could care less if global warming is a natural pattern or man-made. We need to address the issue and find a solution. There's something happening. Whether we're the cause or just the victim of a natural cycle, we have to look at it with a negative slant.

The government has ignored problems in the past with tragic results: People had warned for decades, (that's right, decades), that the levees in New Orleans needed work. Because they never broke before, people ignored the reality until it was too late. It wasn't just in 2005, when Hurricane Katrina hit, that people said, "Hey, the levees are not going to help". People thought the cost has always been too high and it never was deemed necessary. Just like some people still say today about global warming.

[48] I'm not saying you can't be a movie star…okay, I kind of am. The odds are not in your favor. Sue me, I'm a realist.

[49] Thought I forget about that, didn't you? C'mon…admit it. You forgot I was even trying to make a point about global warming.

There are those that say climate change is a natural part of the Earth's lifecycle. They offer evidence showing we've been through these warmer times and that Earth itself can be far more destructive to itself than anything man has created; volcanoes spewing ash and noxious gasses in far higher amounts than factories and automobiles being a prime example. They claim that if we let it run its course everything will work out.

Maybe they are right. Maybe it is a natural process playing out.

Yet even if it is? Is that something we should just let happen? If we can sustain our environment by keeping emissions low, conserving and recycling, why shouldn't we? If we can use this as an excuse to get off our dependency on oil and coal, looking toward cleaner fuels, we should.

I don't want to get all hippy-dippy Earth Day Vegan here…Not every environmentalist is right…Far from it.

We need to look at this with a negative mindset. To see the problems before they happen. To figure out what the worst-case scenario is and plan for it. To ignore the issues and hope for the best, well… good luck with that.

Hope you have floaties and some sunscreen. Or gills.

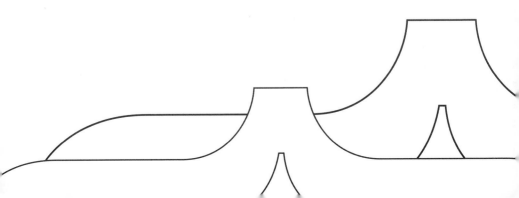

CRAIG PRICE

{ See problems before they arise

Do you see the future? Not literally, but do you often think of the various scenarios and outcomes from a plan like:

What do you do if the economy tanks?

What procedures do you have in place if one of your valued employees left for another opportunity?

Would your family be able to financially recover from your death?

Did I leave the stove on?

Should I get that huge 108 oz. soda right before I go see that four hour epic film?[50]

Am I wearing clean underwear?

If you answered yes to ANY of the above, you're a negative thinker!

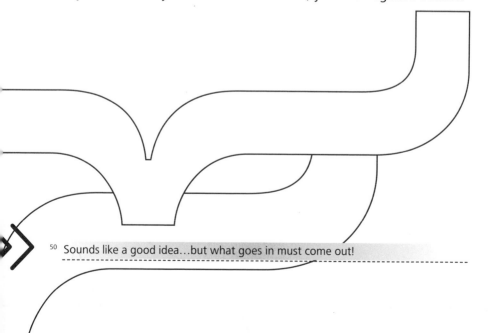

[50] Sounds like a good idea…but what goes in must come out!

DO YOU OWN OR HAVE:

- A fire alarm
- Life insurance
- Car insurance
- Health insurance
- Hell, any insurance whatsoever
- A helmet
- Oven mitts
- A timer
- An alarm clock

- Sunscreen
- Anti-virus software
- A will
- Had vaccinations
- Surge protectors
- Car seats for infants
- Fuse box
- 401k
- Safety deposit box?

These things and much more are all products to prevent or deal with something bad happening. That's right! Negative thinking is everywhere. Even if you don't want to admit it, you use it. Not admitting it is negative thinking! You're protecting yourself from potential ridicule.

This book is a safe place for us, negative thinkers. Feel free to go nuts! Just don't hurt yourself. See, I did it again! This negative thinking can be habit forming.[51]

Do you say "just in case" a lot? Or "on the safe side"? "You never know!"? or "it can't hurt"? These are all phrases said when someone goes the extra step just to be a bit safer, just to avoid problems.

Negative thinkers are often the unsung heroes who save the day by looking into the future to see what could go wrong. Because we are

---

[51] In a good way, like exercise and a balanced diet!

tapping into the negative, we have thought of all the "worst-case scenarios" in advance and have used that information to steer others in a more productive, trouble free direction.

By seeing problems before they happen, we can avoid problems. Those we can't avoid, we can prepare for to lessen the impact.

How can you prepare for possible trouble?

What steps are you going to take to protect your family, business or friends from harm?

What things in your life are dragging you down? Keeping you from succeeding? Wasting your time and resources?

Take the economy of 2008-2009. As the downturn happened, negative thinkers had the assets and liquidity to carry them through the rough patches. They had updated resumes, networked with others, and had their ears to the ground listening for opportunities as well as impending doom so they could jump a sinking ship before the water was over their nose. Never falling into the trap that a good economy will always be there, they are the fabled ant who works throughout the summer, storing food while the positive thinking grasshopper plays, figuring everything will work out in the end.

Can clear, logical decisions go wrong? Of course they can. Taking that brief time to think will reduce the chances of errors.

This stuff isn't magic. It's not some contrived concept that has too many moving parts. Just use it already!

[The Realist's Guidelines]
Hope for the Best, Plan for the Worst

* Don't ask old people "How are you?" unless you're truly prepared to find out.

* Ask yourself the tough questions:
    * What are some things that might cost you down the road?
    * What am I doing with my life, company, relationship that I need to correct?
    * Where am I lacking? Am I missing certain skills that would take me farther than I am today?
    * What is the one thing you can't afford to lose?

* Reality Check: Your innate strengths can only take you so far. To reach your potential you need to identify weaknesses and find solutions to them

* Constantly attempting to be perfect can be a tough way to live your life. You can be happy without being satisfied.

* Know your strengths. Work on your weaknesses.

* Don't be afraid to outsource your weaknesses.

* Negative people see problems before they arise.

* Don't let potential disastrous thoughts overwhelm you. Use them to show you possible outcomes.

FOR THE POSITIVE THINKER:

Keep looking towards the goal. Keep thinking things are going to work out. The world needs people to come up with the exciting, crazy ideas that will change the world. You'll just need some help in the logistical department. You provide the "what" and the "why"; partner up with a negative thinker to get to the "how."

A formidable team has both elements in the right proportion. What that proportion is depends on the team and the desired result. Keep pushing "it can be done!" Be flexible and open to the fact it just might not be the way you envisioned.

CHAPTER 3:

Failure's Success

MAKING MISTAKES IS A PART OF LIFE.

We all make them. You make them, your boss makes them, and your employees make them. Everyone except my wife. I know she doesn't make any because she told me so. Oh, and everything is my fault. I have accepted this truth because I want to remain married and I hate sleeping on the couch. Mistakes are never in short supply.

{ **THE MYTH:** Don't dwell on mistakes. If at first you don't succeed try, try again.

{ **THE REALITY:** Making mistakes is not the problem. Repeating them is. If you constantly repeat the same mistake over and over, you're not learning. If you're not learning, you're not helping.

Mistakes are part of the learning process. Often mistakes show us where we missed something in the planning process. When we make mistakes we need to evaluate what went wrong, not just what went right. After every mistake, it's vital that we sift through the ashes and identify the potential causes.

A mistake is only a problem if you repeat it. Treat your mistakes as learning opportunities. A mistake is a great way of finding out what's not working; a way to self-evaluate your abilities.

No one is perfect. As we strive for perfection, our mistakes will lead the way. How we choose to recover from these mistakes is one of the keys to success.

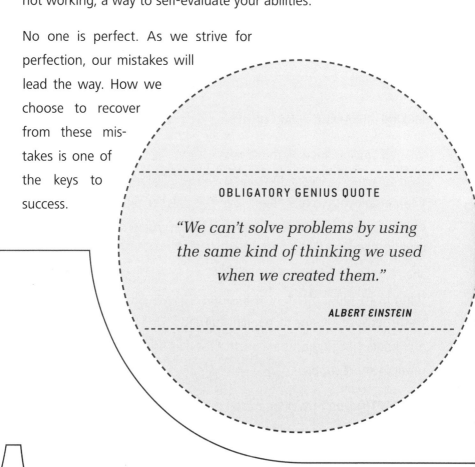

OBLIGATORY GENIUS QUOTE

"We can't solve problems by using the same kind of thinking we used when we created them."

ALBERT EINSTEIN

{ Mastering mistakes

Whenever you commit a mistake it's important you follow these simple steps:

1. Relax

If you make a mistake, calm yourself. When you panic, you make bad decisions.

We hear survival stories all the time, and in them, the ones who don't make it always were the ones who panicked. They didn't think things through and made a series of rash decisions that only got them deeper and deeper in trouble. When you make a mistake, don't panic.

Don't panic!!

Panic causes us to react, not think. Sometimes those reactions are just what the doctor ordered.

Often, they are mindless flailings that end up causing more mistakes. Sometimes, like running out of a burning building, they save your life. As a rule, don't let panic set in.

Relax. Take a calming breath.

You'll need your wits about you to get out of this mess! That's what learning from the mistake is, a second to look back and say, "Whew. Now that it's all over, the chaos and fear of the moment has passed, I can take a calm, realistic look at what happened."

Often we can immediately see what we did wrong, stick that information into the memory banks and move on, knowing we now have one less thing to worry about.

2. Contain

Some mistakes are cut and dry. You made the mistake, it's done, you move on.

Some mistakes are just the beginning. They ripple out and cause more problems until you correct the mistake. You made the mistake and now there are consequences if we don't fix it.

Do your best to stop the forward progression of a snowballing mistake. No need to let it get bigger and more unwieldy. The smaller the mistake, the faster it can be corrected.

Some mistakes are a single instance. Others become a wall of mistakes crashing around you in what I call a "screwnami." Each mistake builds on the previous mistake. We're soon drowning in a sea of missteps that dominate our time and energy correcting.

Slap a bandage on it; apply pressure, whatever you need to do to stop the bleeding. While you may not get a chance to fix the damage already caused, you can prevent it from getting worse.

3. Decide

The fire's out.

The ashes and smoking rubble is all around you.

Time to start repairing the damage.

Now is the time to think your options over. Take some time to decide what's the best way to fix the mistake. Five minutes of planning can save you days of headaches.

Try and take the emotion out of it, because we all get a little scared and nervous when we make a mistake.

Rationally look at the best options. Is there a fix? Can this situation be repaired? What is the next logical action to get back on track? If there isn't one, is there someone I need to apologize to?

Decisions after mistakes can be tricky. You have many options that can have unintended consequences.

4. To confess or not to confess

This one is the toughest for most people. No one likes to admit they screwed up, especially if they can't repair the damage themselves. If you've screwed up at work and haven't found a solution to the problem, confess. Your boss may be able to save the day!

Oddly enough, even though you may think many managers and bosses were promoted because of incompetency, most have been in your position before they were promoted. They've been in your shoes, maybe even made the same mistake you've made and they might have the answer just sitting in their pocket waiting for the day that mistake is made by someone else. Their experience with the situation could be the bailout you're looking for.

If you're a boss and you've made that mistake, let them know. It takes a huge burden off of them, to say, "Hey, we've all been there, let's get this fixed right now."

If you do confess, don't lie or try to cover-up your involvement.

Lies and cover-up will almost always backfire. Time is not on your side. Sooner or later someone will find out.

The first time you're caught in a lie will be the last time those people will ever trust you. Besides, lies are tough to keep going because they require you to remember everything.

You don't need to remember the truth, but a lie you need to remember.

If you've ever watched one of the thirteen *Law and Order* shows, they always interrogate people to find inconsistencies. Ask the question three different times, and get three different answers.

Lying!

Your hard earned credibility is lost too easily by lying and can be extremely difficult to repair.

Don't risk it.

That doesn't mean you have to confess every time.

I know what you're thinking:

Wait! You just told me to confess. Now I've just screwed myself by spilling my guts!

Well, life isn't a series of simple steps. We need to think about what we do. Sorry, a realist understands there is more than one solution to most problems.

There are going to be times you don't need to confess. If you can fix the problem quickly and quietly, then do so. No harm, no foul.

Often, people like to over-confess; tell all the problems or mistakes they've created so they can present themselves as problem solvers.

"Look! I screwed up so bad, but thanks to my superior intellect and keen reactions, I was able to correct it without any help!" translates into "I'm a big screw-up, don't leave me alone with sharp objects."

You don't need to tell people about every mistake. With the ones that get out of your control, go get some help.

5. Keep it real

Be objective about the seriousness of your mistakes.

Don't over or under value those mistakes. Take the serious ones seriously and the little ones in stride. Look at every mistake and judge it honestly.

Was it a serious mistake that could have hurt someone? Then regardless of how quickly or effectively it was handled, regardless of the fact that no one did get hurt, take it seriously.

If you make a huge, monumental mistake that freaks everyone out and you just go "Meh" and think nothing of it again, someone in a position of authority may think it's a real big deal and your nonchalant attitude will only piss them off. Nothing irritates a person faster than when they think something is important and you don't.

Was it a minor mistake that was easily handled?

People often blow little mistakes way out of proportion. They turn it into a morality play of life and death. They want to show how much they care by making it sound like it was the biggest mistake in the history of the world.

We know you care. You don't need to exaggerate to show how invested you are. We know every day, because we see how you act. Your character defines you, not necessarily your mistakes.

Don't condemn yourself with simple mistakes that happen.

Too often, people burden themselves with frivolous mistakes, causing major self-esteem issues and poor self-images. Dwelling on the mistake eats at you. It's important you take responsibility and own the mistake, just don't look at it as a soul-devouring episode. It's a moment to educate yourself and make yourself a better person.

There are enough valid things we do that cause low self-esteem, let's not add more to the pile!

Which leads us to:

6. Everyone meks missteakes.

You do it. I do it. We all screw up from time to time. You're not unique in your occasional ineptitude.[52] Most people make minor mistakes all the time. It's part of the human experience.

If you don't make mistakes, you're not trying hard enough. Everyone makes mistakes. Some of you are thinking reading this book was one of them.[53]

Once you understand mistakes are a part of life, the fear of making them should diminish.

Go out and make a few, a little one here and there, then graduate to big ones! The sooner you can learn to master mistakes, the less often you'll actually make them. Because taking the fear out of mistakes, no longer makes it a mistake, just another opportunity to learn.

[52] Well, maybe YOU are.

[53] If that's the case, I hope for my sake you paid in cash and lost your receipt!

Wow, that sounds almost like a cheesy motivational poster!

Sorry, my mistake.

{ Famous failures

A mistake can sometimes turn into a real failure. Failure is a mistake taken to the next level. Failures can rarely be corrected. You usually have to start all over with a failure. Even when we fail, we can learn. Sometimes there are unintended results that have value. Sometimes the outcome is nothing close to what we wanted, yet be entirely more useful than we ever would have imagined. Often failures make us re-assess how we are doing something, forcing us to do things we hadn't planned, that turn out to be improvements.

OBLIGATORY FAMOUS
EMANCIPATOR QUOTE

"My great concern is not whether you have failed, but whether you are content with your failure."

ABRAHAM LINCOLN

Never look at failure as an ending. Like its little brother the mistake, failure is a great way to exceed your own limited expectations. The following are just a few examples of when a bad idea goes good!

SILLY PUTTY

Silly putty was discovered during World War II, thanks to a failure to create a rubber replacement. While mixing chemicals in a lab, James Wright, working for General Electric, combined boric acid and silicone oil. This did not create rubber. In fact, it really only created creepy flesh colored lumps of stuff that had no real applicable use. Never one to let a failure go to waste, GE sent out the compound to researchers to see if they could find any kind of real use for it.

Sadly, to the dismay of GE shareholders, they couldn't use it for anything productive. Probably because the researchers were too busy playing with it all the time. One of these researchers, Dr. Earl Warwick, took the compound and again, trying to create a synthetic rubber, instead created a more bouncy version of the original compound. Again, nothing useful could be made with the "nutty putty" as they called it, but the guys in the lab just loved playing with it.

Finally, in 1949, a marketing person named Peter Hodgsen saw the possibilities for the putty as a children's toy, and came up with the name Silly Putty, thanks to its main ingredient silicone. I'm still not sure how these adults were able to play with this stuff for hours, yet it became a huge success.

For decades, children have used silly putty as their own personal comic photocopier and as projectiles to throw at other children.[54]

---

[54] I always thought it was just what plastic surgeons used to fill any unfortunate gaps, since it looks oddly similar to Joan Rivers' skin.

Failure can be devastating if you let it. More so if you don't expect it. Other times it can be downright silly. Looking for other uses from failure can lead to huge successes.

CORN FLAKES

I love corn flakes. Absolutely love them! Especially Kellogg's Frosted Flakes. Did you know it was created out of failure and desperation? It was a combination of small budget and bad cooking that led to this wonderful breakfast cereal.

Dr. John Harvey Kellogg and his brother Will Keith were cooking at the Battle Creek Sanitarium when some more important matter pulled both of them away from the wheat they were processing. While they ran off to attend whatever issue they had,[55] the wheat became stale. Being short of time and money, they decided to use the supposedly ruined wheat and attempted to flatten the dough into sheets to minimize their losses. Instead of dough they got flakes. Toasted, tasty flakes. They served the flakes with milk and marshmallows, which became a very popular food among the patients. The brothers then experimented with other flakes from other grains.

Considering what Dr. Kellogg was usually serving his patients, a daily dose of enemas and yogurt,[56] you could see how they'd prefer the tasty flakes. A cost cutting measure from a mistake created a tasty breakfast for you and for me. Sometimes mistakes are like happy little accidents. Don't look at mistakes as horrible problems (though they can be and often are). Learn from them, see it there is any use from the mistake and move on.

---

[55] Probably a patient having an episode complaining about the lack of a good breakfast!

[56] Mmmm…sounds yummy doesn't it? I'm walking bowlegged just thinking about it.

SCOTCHGARD

Oddly enough, Scotchgard is not the name of the lock on a liquor cabinet. There really is nothing Scottish about it either. In fact, even the word guard is misspelled! With all these apparent flaws, Scotchgard became a huge success simply because someone was paying attention when something went amiss.

Patsy Sherman was a research chemist for 3M in the 1950's. While working in the lab one day, an accidental spill brought 3M some valuable results. I'll let Patsy explain in her own words:

"We were trying to develop a new kind of rubber for jet aircraft fuel lines, when one of the lab assistants accidentally dropped a glass bottle that contained a batch of synthetic latex I had made. Some of the latex mixture splashed on the assistant's canvas tennis shoes and the result was remarkable."[57]

Remarkable in the fact that they had created a substance that didn't wash off, didn't come off with any solvents and didn't allow anything else to stain the area where it had landed on the shoes. Even a researcher could see the marketing and commercial potential of a substance that allowed fabrics to be stain resistant and thus, Scotchgard was created.

The next time I spill something, I'll be sure to remind my wife that it could very well be the first step to our vast fortune.[58]

Now if only it could apply to politicians' reputations… we could call it ScumGard.

---

[57] Mary Bellis. (n.d.). "The Invention of Scotchgard". Retrieved 08 21, 2006, from About.com: http://inventors.about.com/library/inventors/blscotchgard.htm

[58] Somehow, I think I'll still get in trouble.

KRAZY GLUE

Here's a failure that not only is useful, it has saved lives. Superglue and Krazy glue is really Cyanoacrylate. Sounds kind of dangerous, doesn't it? Yet this failure has helped millions of people.

It all started when Harry Coover at Eastman Kodak was looking to find a way to make extra-clear plastic gun sights during World War II. Instead of a nice clear plastic, he accidentally created a clear glue. Really good glue. Some might even say this glue was "super." It proved to be a huge misfortunate fortune in more ways than the marketing people would let on.

Instead of any practical application for a weapon, Eastman Kodak immediately could see its potential in the aftermath from a weapon. They could see how the glue could be applied to stop bleeding and keep wounds closed in emergency situations. Good old Eastman Kodak, if they can't kill you, they'll keep you alive long enough so someone else can.

Years later, during the Vietnam War, testing was supposedly done in the field, despite failing to get FDA approval due to it causing skin irritation and generating heat.[59]

"If somebody had a chest wound or open wound that was bleeding, the biggest problem they had was stopping the bleeding so they could get the patient back to the hospital. And the consequence was—many of them bled to death. The medics used the spray, stopped the bleeding, and were able to get the wounded back to the base hospital. And many, many lives were saved. " — Dr. Harry Coover[60]

---

[59] Seems kind of mild in today's world where we see advertisements for headache medications whose side effects include bleeding, upset stomach, diarrhea, ulcers, anal seepage, heart attack and death. I think I'll just have the headaches, thank you!

[60] Hayes, Sharon Caskey."Discovery of Super Glue helped land Coover in National Inventors Hall of Fame", Kingsport Times-News, July 11, 2004.

Eventually in the late 1990's a medically safe version of this strong glue was created. It also has found a use in criminal forensics to recover latent fingerprints. Of course, there is the fact it is exceptional glue.

In 1959, Coover was a guest on the television show "I've Got a Secret," with host Garry Moore. He put one drop of glue in between two steel cylinders and counted to 10. The bonded steel was used to lift Moore several feet off the floor. He said the bonded steel would lift up to 3,000 pounds after just 10 seconds, and it would eventually hold at least 5,000 pounds.

Sometimes, failures seem totally unrelated to what we are trying to accomplish. By looking at our failures, other uses, other products can be discovered. Always look back at your failures. Though you may not have reached your goal, a whole other set of goals may appear. Just *stick* to it![61]

POST-IT NOTES

There are often times when we set out to achieve something and the results are "less than satisfactory," to put it nicely. Just because it's not the pinnacle of perfection doesn't mean it can't be extremely useful.

In 1968, Spencer Silver of 3M was to develop a strong adhesive. Instead, he came up with something rather weak. Sure it stuck, but then it easily became unstuck. I think spitting on the back of a piece of paper was just as effective.

For years, Spencer tried to sell this not-so-sticky glue but found no interest. That was until a colleague, Alan Fry, thought it might be use-

[61] Sorry, it was a softball. I had to do it.

ful to keep bookmarks in his hymn book. After developing this new idea further, he convinced 3M to make the product you have today, Post-it Notes. Used in offices practically everywhere, its initial launch was another lesson in dealing with failure.

The first year on the market was just miserable for the Post-it. No one knew what the heck it was or what it was for, so no one bought them. 3M realized that the reason the product failed was lack of consumer education. They decided to test market them by giving away free samples. Once people saw their use, the product took off.

Sometimes we don't reach our goals. Sometimes the outcome is less than we expected. That doesn't make it a failure. By using what you've got, instead of throwing it all away and starting over…it might be more useful than you intended!

VIAGRA

Sometimes, we're working on a project and it succeeds, maybe just not as well as we would like. In fact, while the project we're working on proves to be successful, it may actually be more useful for something else. Like Viagra.

Viagra started out as Sildenafil (compound UK-92,480), a hopeful remedy for hypertension and angina. Apparently it didn't really do much for angina during testing. They quickly they discovered that it had other…uh…well…uplifting properties.[62]

Sure, it didn't stop a heart attack, who cares? An erection in a pill is something we can sell!!

[62] I'm not sure how they found out about this side-effect. I guess the guys in those patient gowns kept knocking cups off the night stand or something.

Like life, sometimes we don't get the result we want. If we take the time to look at what happened, it could still be useful to us.

Actually, Viagra has several uses. My favorite? A low-concentration solution of sildenafil in water significantly prolongs the time before cut flowers wilt; one experiment showed a doubling in time from one week to two weeks.[63]

And really...isn't that what Viagra is for?

Wilt prevention.

COLUMBUS DAY

As far as Americans are concerned, let's talk about the most important failure of all: Christopher Columbus!

Columbus Day is a day to celebrate man's refusal to ask for directions, a day to celebrate someone "discovering" a place where people already live, a place that was actually discovered hundreds of years earlier by someone else. Proof that even major screw-ups, given enough time, can be recovered from. It is the most screwed up holiday of all!

Columbus' voyages across the Atlantic Ocean has been heralded as the birth of the New World, European colonization of the west and pretty much the landmark we use to judge all explorers. While history claims he discovered America on his first voyage of 1492, he did not actually reach the mainland until his third voyage in 1498! He discovered the island which is now the Bahamas accidentally while trying to find an alternative route to India, which is why Native Americans are called "Indians."

[63] Paul Simons, "Viagra Gives Plants a Lift," *The Guardian*, 9/12/2002.

Never mind the fact he was not even the first European to reach the Americas. Many historians give that distinction to Norseman Leif Erikson.[64]

Now every October you can celebrate one of the most fortunate failures in American history. Fortunate for everyone except perhaps the Native Indians. They didn't fare so well once the settlers came.

But, hey, let's not let that ruin a day off.

ARTIFICIAL SWEETENERS

People always assume you have to do things a certain way to be successful. Artificial sweeteners are great examples of how bad lab practices and missteps turned into success.

First, there is Saccharin. Sometime in 1879, a professor at John Hopkins University, Ira Remsen and his research associate, Constantin Fahlberg, discovered the chemical while working with coal tar. Both men tasted the residue of the sweet substance on their hands thanks to their apparent complete lack of hygiene. Their separate but similar failures to keep a clean environment lead to a huge discovery.

It seems not washing ones hands is pretty common, especially among men. More specifically, among men who are scientists. That's how we got Nutrasweet!

Nutrasweet is made from Aspartame.[65] Aspartame was discovered when the chemist, James Schlatter with G.D. Searle & Company, was

---

[64] Not to be confused with Leif Garrett, who discovered that drugs and a bad singing career rarely end well.

[65] That is not a swear word.

concocting an anti-ulcer drug. Without thinking, he licked his finger, which had been accidentally contaminated with Aspartame.

Sometimes, discoveries happen from simple communication errors, the way Sucralose (or Splenda, as it is also known as) was discovered.

Sucralose was discovered in 1976 by scientists from Tate & Lyle, working with researchers Leslie Hough and Shashikant Phadnis. While working in the lab one day, Hough handed Phandis some powder they were working on and asked Phandis to "Test this." Phandis heard "taste this" and like any good lab researcher, when some dude hands you funky powder and say "Hey man...taste this!" you immediately comply. Of course the powder was super sweet and the rest is sugar substitute history.

So what have we learned?

Scientists are gross.

True.

They will put things in their mouth without question and won't wash their hands (a very bad combo). We also learned we need to be open to unexpected results. Failure is often the first step to success. Even if that success is not what you planned it to be!

CELLOPHANE

Good idea...bad execution.

Cellophane was invented by a Swiss chemist named Jacques E. Brandenberger when he got the notion of creating a cloth that repelled liquids instead of absorbing them. He created a waterproof spray

made from viscose that he then covered the cloth with. Problem was, it was far too stiff. Luckily, he realized the coating could easily peel off the cloth as a clear film. This new discovery had more obvious applications, so he abandoned his original idea of a water-repellant fabric to focus on this material.

Sometimes what we hope to accomplish turns into something totally different. We need to be open to new thoughts, new ideas, new goals, and new successes. A good failure can do that for us.

SAFETY GLASS

Sometimes we make simple mistakes. We forget something or over-look a step in a process. It happens. Sometimes it leads to trouble. Other times…

In 1903 Edouard Benedictus was mixing chemicals in his laboratory, like any other day. His assistant emptied a beaker, but instead of cleaning the beaker, the assistant put it on the shelf. A couple of weeks later, Benedictus accidentally dropped the beaker on the floor. Instead of glass smashing all over the place, the glass stayed in a clump. Thankfully, the assistant proved more useful with his documentation skills than his cleaning abilities because he kept a record of what had been in the broken beaker and they were able to perfect safety glass.

Before safety glass, if you got in a car accident, you flew through the windshield and came out the other side shredded wheat. Now, you just bounce your head off the glass. Sure it still hurts, but it's much less traumatic to the body. Just think, millions of lives saved because someone forgot to clean a beaker.

Now this would not be tolerated in today's super strict, safety conscious laboratories, or at least I hope not. Always be on the lookout after a failure. Be open to the failure and the information it will give you. You might just invent something that will save millions of lives. Or it will, at the least, remind you to wash chemicals from beakers!

CORONARY CATHETERIZATION

Have you ever totally messed something up? I mean completely missed the mark and made a huge mistake? We all have. Sometimes major mistakes lead to major discoveries, like coronary catheterization. For those of you who don't know (I was one of them), coronary catheterization is another term for angiogram. They run a thin flexible tube into the heart and inject dye to look for blockages. How fun! It was a little mishap that spawned the idea.

A pediatric cardiologist at the Cleveland Clinic accidentally injected radiocontrast in the coronary artery instead of the left ventricle.[66] Although the patient had a reversible cardiac arrest, Sones and Shirey developed the procedure further and are credited with the discovery.

Sure he caused a reversible cardiac arrest. Who hasn't? Yet he learned from his mistake, saw something of value in his actions and it is now used to treat and diagnose heart issues. His one major mistake has probably saved thousands of lives.

Don't rake yourself over the coals when you do make a mistake. If you learn from them, they no longer become mistakes but opportunities to learn.

[66] Repeat that sentence at dinner parties if you want to sound super-smart!

JAWS

Steven Spielberg has always been a director I have admired. His ability to craft a film has few, if any, equals. One of the most famous Hollywood failures sent him skyrocketing from "talented young director" to "master of the art." No, it was not '1941'.

It was, in fact, *Jaws*.

Jaws? The movie that made almost $470 million worldwide is a failure? The movie *Jaws* that invented the "blockbuster" title, an utter disaster? Uh…no.

Multiple failures during the production of the movie made it even better than planned. Who is the main culprit of this failure? A shark named Bruce.

Bruce the Mechanical Shark is not unlike many Hollywood megastars…moody, uncooperative, and demanding of attention. It is the fact that Bruce the Mechanical Shark failed continuously that led to the changes that made Jaws such a special movie.

The script was refined during production, and the unreliable mechanical sharks forced Spielberg to shoot most of the scenes with the shark only hinted at. For example, for much of the shark hunt its location is represented by the floating yellow barrels. This forced restraint is widely thought to have increased the suspense of these scenes, giving it a Hitchcockian tone.[67]

What a fortunate misfortune! By adapting and changing his goals to fit the reality of the situation in front of him, Spielberg was cornered

---

[67] Harvey, Neil (2005-06-13). "30 years of 'Jaws'". The Roanoke Times. http://www.roanoke.com/extra%5C25348.html. Retrieved 2010-03-12

into rethinking shot selections, or other ways of telling the same story with the limited resources he had available to him.

We sometimes need to accept failures as steering mechanisms. Look for alternatives to your goal. There is never one way to get something done. While we may not like to admit it, sometimes our original plan isn't nearly as good as our back-up.

INDIANA JONES

By now we all know how failures can point you toward success. Still unconvinced?

I give you: Indiana Jones. Arguably the best hero in cinema history and in my opinion the reason scruffy beards are socially acceptable, occasionally fashionable. One of the more memorable moments in *"Raiders of the Lost Ark"* happened because of a breakdown.

Indiana Jones was a charismatic rogue that carried a whip, though we never saw him use it very much in Raiders. Why? Well, the day of the big whip/knife battle was to be shot on the set between Harrison Ford and some sword wielding villain in the middle of a village, Harrison was overcome with dysentery. Sweating and cramping, Harrison looked at the director Steven Spielberg and asked "Why don't we just shoot the sucker?" Spielberg, with orders from producer George Lucas to be on time and under budget, saw an opportunity to shoot two birds with one stone (and a villain), agreed, scrapped the rest of the fight scene, and filmed the gag of Indiana quickly shooting the swordsman.

Life is not perfect. You have to work with what you've got, and be flexible at all times. Like Indy!

POTATO CHIPS

This failure originated from spite. Spite is a pretty bad thing. I would hope you don't do anything out of spite. We all have weak moments when our anger lashes out to other people. If we can learn from them, then something worthwhile can be gained. Look at George Crum.

George is the inventor of the original potato chip recipe. Working at Moon's Lake House in Saratoga Springs, NY, George became more than a bit irritated with a customer who kept sending back his fried potatoes for being too thick and soggy. Crum figured he'd show this customer who's the chef in his kitchen and sliced the returned potatoes so thin, fried them so much that the customer would be left in stunned silence. Thankfully, something else altogether unexpected happen. The customer loved them! They became a huge hit and were a regular on the menu.

George's diabolical plan to get back at a customer blew up in his face. Thankfully! What would the world be without Pringles??

It would be a sad, sad, unsalted world, that's what.

TELEPHONES

This little blunder is what I like to call Found in Translation. Sometimes misinterpretations allow us to move forward. Take the case of Alexander Graham Bell. Before he invented the telephone, he studied transmitting tones electronically.

One of the key people that caught Bell's imagination was physicist Hermann Von Helmholtz, who wrote that vowel sounds could be created with electric tuning forks and resonators. One slight problem for

Bell caused a slight, yet fortunate problem. Bell couldn't read German. He mistranslated that vowel sounds could be transmitted over wire. Hermann said no such thing but Bell was none the wiser.

He would later say of this misunderstanding, "It gave me confidence. If I had been able to read German, I might never have begun my experiments in electricity."

Soon he was transmitting sounds via electricity over wire.

Sometimes mistakes can build some false confidence that allows you to take a step you may not have taken. Some false confidence is good. Some can get you into trouble. Being able to balance it is the key to success.

Mistakes happen every day. Are you doing your best to make something out of them?

PACEMAKERS

A simple mistake can show us something we never expected.

Wilson Greatbatch was working as a medical researcher in the late 1950s. As he was building an oscillator to record heart sounds, he accidentally put in one of the resistors with the wrong resistance. It gave off a rhythmic electric pulse, almost like a heartbeat. In fact, after a few years of perfecting this new pulsing device, he had the world's first implantable pacemaker. Up until then, they used machines as big as an industrial microwave, which were quite painful to the patient.

All Wilson was trying to do was record sound. Instead he improved and prolonged the lives of millions of people. Mistakes are about learning. It's how we grow and improve. If we can keep our mind open and sharp enough when we make our mistakes, we can often surge ahead with the new information we learned from our failure.

It is a good thing mistakes happen every day for most of us!

{ Failure is not an option

As you can see for yourself, making mistakes and failing is not necessarily the end of the world. It's often one of the many steps to success and more informative than succeeding.

You can never be sure what is working until it breaks down, exposing the true worth of an idea, a part, a person or a plan.

It always tickles me when someone cries out "Failure is NOT an option!" This is true. It's not an option, it's a result. Not necessarily the final result but a result, nonetheless.

Every failure offers up an opportunity to learn. You can only truly learn by looking back at what went wrong. Never be afraid to look back and use failure as a launching point for something better. Or at least an object lesson in what not to do again!

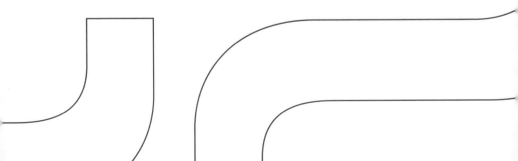

{ Isn't that special?

Another thing about failure: Many people claim failures are due to someone's fear of success. People are not afraid of succeeding. They are more afraid of failing in front of a larger audience. The more you succeed, the more people notice when you screw up. Or at least we like to think more people are watching. Most likely they're not. We feel "special" in our minds so people must be interested in my life.

If everyone is special, doesn't that make being special lose its power? Aren't most people similar? I mean if you're a one-in-a-million type of person that means there are currently 6600 people just like you. And 301 of them live here in America.

All this specialness gives people the feeling that if you don't treat them special you are disrespecting them.

Respect and being "special" is not a birthright, it is something earned. What have you done to earn respect? What have you done to be special?

Being born doesn't make you special. Too many people do it every day. Working, living, being is not enough to be special. I hope you strive to be special, just don't fall into the pitfall of feeling special.

Vanity is not a good look for most people. Self-esteem is great in the right dose. Negative thinking, like positive thinking, needs a balance.

I believe many people desperately try to show their uniqueness. They want to be special. Sadly they do this by acting like other people.

All the tattoo artists talk about each tattoo being unique, yet if you just look at people with tattoos and their tattoos themselves, they all start to look similar. They may be trying to show how they are individuals. By becoming more androgynous and monochromatic?

About those people just like you. More often than not, if you ever get a chance to meet one of these people just like you, you won't like them. Probably because they think they're special and they're not.

All this talk about "Fear of Success" is insane. Very rarely does someone not want more money, more power, more adoration. What they don't want to do is get more money, more power and more adoration only to lose it because they failed.

Now, you don't need to fear failure and we don't need to fear success. All we have to fear now is serial killers in your closets and catching something via public toilets!

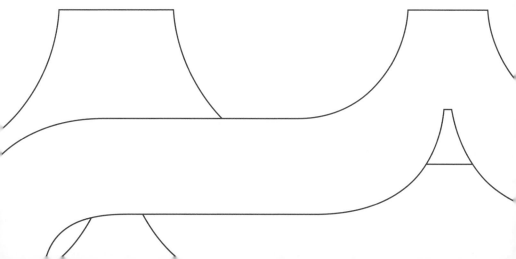

[Realist's Guidelines]
Failure's Success

✱ Making mistakes is not the problem. Repeating them is.

✱ After you make a mistake:
  * Relax
  * Contain
  * Decide
  * Confess or Not
  * Keep it real
  * Remember that everyone makes mistakes

✱ Even if you fail, you can learn.

✱ Reality Check: Back in the day, scientists were really gross.

✱ Viagra causes erections.[68]

---

[68] That's the side-effect!!!

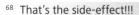

FOR THE POSITIVE THINKERS:

Look at mistakes and failures like Bob Ross from "The Joy of Painting" did. They were always happy accidents that became part of the final painting, something to be embraced instead of corrected or erased. These little accidents spice up your life and add a little unexpected adrenaline!

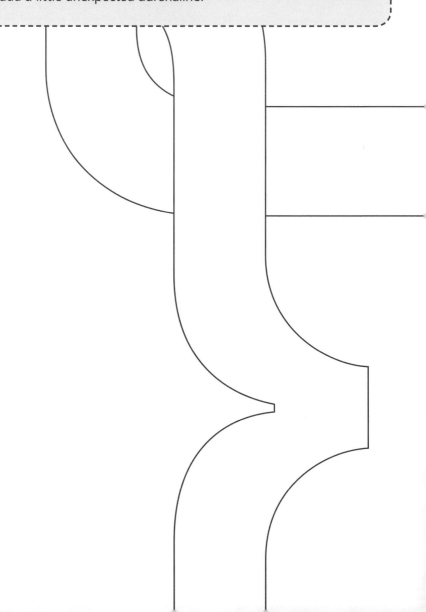

CHAPTER 4:

Complainers, Complaints and Objections

I AM SO SICK OF COMPLAINERS. AREN'T YOU? DON'T THEY JUST IRRITATE YOU TO THE VERY BONE? I CAN'T BELIEVE THEY CAN JUST WHINE AND MOAN ABOUT EVERYTHING WITHOUT AN END IN SIGHT.

Complainers are such big … oh. Wait a second. Am I complaining about complaining? Looks like it to me!

There is no getting around it. Complaints and complainers are everywhere. I complain. You complain. If you don't complain, check your pulse.

We all, at one point or another, complain, some more than others, some even more than that. It's our ability to understand the complainer's point of view and the reason for the complaints that will make life a tad smoother.

Are you willing to take the time to differentiate between a whiner and a complainer?

THE MYTH: Complainers have nothing of value to add; they just want to shoot every good idea down.

THE REALITY: Complainers are usually people with opposing viewpoints who sincerely want you to avoid a mistake that could cause damage.

HOW TO SPOT A WHINER:

1. Whiners, as a matter of definition, whine. The sound like pouty, spoiled children[69] who haven't gotten their way. Huffing and puffing, tsking a lot and sighing heavily, all for dramatic effect.

2. They treat every issue like a personal attack. If a rule that applies to everyone is put in place, they look at it as if they are being singled out; regardless of how little they were involved in the creation of the rule.

3. They constantly repeat their problem, unprompted and without context. You're talking about how the heat is too high in the office, they immediately bring up how their neighbors dog is always going on their lawn. If you have to look at someone and ask "What the hell are you talking about?" Ding-ding-ding! We have a whiner!

4. Their reasoning is not based in any kind of earthly logic. This is usually the main difference between a whiner and a complainer. A whiner consistently has no real reason to complain other than

---

[69] They probably were which is why they are whining. Reality finally caught up to their parent-protected bubble.

to vocalize their need for attention. They bring up wild, one-in-a-million, unrealistic excuses to stall, stop or plain ruin a plan. Why? With irrational people you can never tell. All you can be sure of is, to them, its life threatening.

WARNING:

When ignored, complainers can readily transform into whiners.

OBLIGATORY ROCK STAR *QUOTE*

"I can't complain, but sometimes I still do."

JOE WALSH

{ Don't disregard the message because you don't like the messenger

Whiners are like vampires.

Until you drive a stake through the heart of the complaint, they just won't … shut … up! They keep coming back like a bad horror movie.

What we need to realize is that complaints almost always have a kernel of truth to them. It could be a tiny speck of truth and, through their egos, exaggeration or any number of other reasons; the whiner has inflated that speck into a complaint. If it doesn't have any truth in it, it's what we call "a bald face lie." That's a totally different situation. If we can identify the reason for the kernel, we put a stake in it and deflate it out of existence, or at least turn it into something more manageable. Here is the best way to slay the complaining "undead" of the real world.

Listen.

Being able to identify the kernel of truth is the trick.

Sometimes it's a small problem that only affects the person making the complaint. Maybe it's easily fixable, maybe not. Either way, the whiner wants to be heard. So listen.

Try not to react to the complaint by playing "Counterpoint" and showing how invalid their complaint actually is.

Defending our positions while people complain usually causes the complaints to escalate. People will exaggerate more and more to show you just how important whatever the gripe is to them. They need to compensate for the lack of attention by making the truth seem so much more important. Soon that complaint becomes this unwieldy, out of control avalanche of anxiety and stress for everyone in the area.

The easiest solution is to simply take five minutes out of your day and listen to them. Sit them down and find out the problem. Don't judge, at least not while you're talking to them.[70]

By really listening to the complaint,[71] you can usually find the reason for its existence.

Recognize.

Sometimes the complaint is just a way for the person to feel heard. They want someone to say, "You are so right. Thank God you spoke up and saved the company. I find you a valuable and worthy employee. Here's a raise!"

Well, maybe that's just me. The point is still valid. When you take the time to listen to them, try and see it from their perspective. It's extremely hard for people to see another point of view, but make the effort. They don't have to be right, but you can look at why they might have a complaint.

People look for understanding more than anything. Does that mean you're going to fix the problem? Not necessarily.

---

[70] Rolling your eyes as they talk is a big no-no. Save the judging for when you are alone or at least away from them where they can't hear you giggle.

[71] I know, I hate doing that too!

Solve the problem.

This can be tricky, because sometimes it's a fundamental problem that has been overlooked and the individual is trying to warn others. Sometimes it's a problem only in the warped mind of the whiner. It's your job to figure out the validity and importance of the complaint.

Get past all the emotion and irritation the complainer has and locate their truth. Don't just dismiss the problem.

Often personality gets in the way and the complaint from the grumpy, obnoxious guy in the cubicle on the end[72] is ignored.

Try not to ignore the message just because you don't like the messenger or the messenger's delivery. Many huge corporate mistakes were known about in advance and ignored. The fact that a complainer identified it caused it to be dismissed. He or she may have some very valid points that make a great deal of sense.

Don't fall into the trap of dismissing the cry of "the sky is falling" until you get hit in the head with a piece of ceiling. Some problems are easier than others. By solving the issue, we remove the kernel of truth to the complaint, rendering it moot. Once you solve the problem what do they have to complain about? To be honest, complainers are really good at complaining so even if you solve the problem, they'll probably complain about the fact that it took so much time to solve their complaint.

"I can't believe how long it took them to figure out just how right I was!" Over time that complaint will deflate. Solving a legitimate problem can make the complaining disappear immediately.

---

[72] You know, the guy you wait for to go to the bathroom so you can sneak out and go to lunch without having to ask him to go, too.

People often think whiners are socially awkward losers. Actually, many of them have friends. They go to lunch every day with others and they usually complain to them, too. Like vampires, whiners, left to their own devices, will bite others, suck the life out of them and ultimately make them part of their brood. Soon, the person is brainwashed into thinking the complainer may have a point.

You start with one complainer, then he infects another, those two infect two more people and you can do the math. Next thing you know, you have a coven of complaining vampires turning everyone against the boss.

An effective complainer can contaminate and destroy morale. If they slowly infect the coworkers around them, you soon will have a serious problem that no amount of Holy Water can fix. You can also use this converting power to your advantage.

{ Converting vampires

You can use the complainer as a Public Address system.

If you have a good complainer, they usually are not very shy about sharing their opinions or complaints. Basically, you are going to get the vampire to work for you instead of against you.

If you have a new policy or a new idea, before you implement it, find your complainer, or as I like to call them "The Mouth." Every person knows "the mouth", that one person who talks to everybody.

They can be nice and hard working yet somehow, through guile and sheer personality have some influence over the masses.

Now you're going to do something you may not want to do, but it's something you need to do. Try being more inclusive and ask for their opinions ahead of time (even if they are wrong 99% of the time). By getting them involved (even superficially) early on in the process, it makes them feel part of the decision making process and they feel more valuable and more willing to accept the decision.

Who would *poo-poo* their own idea? The other great thing about getting a complainer's feedback early is that they can really rip an idea to shreds. Remember, you don't have to listen or do everything they say, but they may spot flaws you never considered. Use that to improve.

Once you have the idea ready to be implemented, you can unleash the mouth on the rest of the team. You won them over, now they will be much more supportive because they feel like they own a part of it. They will defend the idea from others. Now your vampire is turning everyone on to your side. It's an invaluable way of implementing new rules, new procedures and avoiding unnecessary conflict.

{ Squeaky wheels

There are those few people who feel complaining is the only way they can be heard. They're true believers in "the squeaky wheel gets the grease."

These squeaky wheels complain and complain, often getting what they want, irritating the rest of us. They use this acquiescence as justification to complain all the time. Occasionally, the squeaky wheel gets re-placed. It's a ratio of talent to tolerance. Before you take to com-plaining, young padawan, ask yourself, "Am I talented enough to be tolerated? "

If you're not - your antics won't be tolerated either. Do you bring enough to the table to act like a jerk? True jerks will answer with "yes, I am." Although the reality is that often the answer is "No. No you are not. Don't let the door hit ya where the good Lord split ya!"

We've already discussed how valuable a tool *complaining* can be – but only if done properly. Whining is not - even if done to perfection. Are you sabotaging yourself with your mouth? Are you complaining to the wrong people? At the wrong time? Too often?

Complain up.
Complaints should be aimed at people who can do something about them. Not at other people who feel the same irritation and especially not to subordinates who look to you to fix things.

This is just like the old expression about smiling monkeys in a tree. "When you look down the organizational chart (the tree) from above, you should see smiling monkeys, and those at the bottom look up and see…" well you can figure out the rest.[73]

Be careful complaining farther up the ladder than you should. Noth-ing will alienate and irritate your boss than going over their head. The point is you should complain to your boss, not to your employees.

[73] If you don't know, email me at Craig@SpeakerCraigPrice.com Hint: It's a swear word! Insert childish giggle!

Complain in private.

Once you find the right person to file your complaint with, don't go public with it.

Meetings and company parties are not the place to bring up complaints. If you want something fixed, publicly cornering someone rarely turns out in your best interest.

Complain once.

Constant harping is for angels. And you're not dead yet.

Prepare your complaint ahead of time, unleash its elegance and import and then move on. Or at least give it some space. The more often you complain, the more you become white noise, blending into the background, losing credibility with each warning, each important piece of friendly advice.

It can turn into a classic case of "The Boy Who Called Wolf Syndrome." When you really have a point, something vital to say, it will be lost because people tuned you out.

You need to ask yourself, "Am I valuable enough to make everyone else miserable with my complaints?" Odds are you're not. If you keep it up, you can be replaced with a younger, less expensive squeak-free wheel.

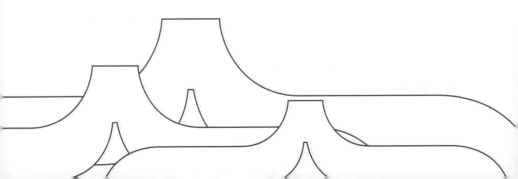

{ Dealing with objections

They say necessity is the mother of invention. Negativity is its father.

Innovation sometimes comes about by seeing something wrong with an existing product, or maybe it's lacking in one area and improving on it.

Improvement is inherently negative. Improvements don't usually happen if something works great. You find the flaw and make it better. While the end result is positive, the impetus[74] is due to negative thinking.

It works the same at the office. Positive thinkers say "I love working here at Company X. It's the best place I've ever worked. Don't change a thing!"

Negative thinkers say "I love working here at Company X. It's the best place I've ever worked. It would be even better if we…" Finding the weak spots and making them stronger, that's how work improves, how life improves, how everything improves!

Change is going to happen. Before you change something, ask around. See what the reactions will be to the change. Everyone will complain, because we fear change, but listen to the complaints.

Separate the actual problems from the unwarranted anxieties. Usually you can find an easier way to implement the change. The complaints may highlight major issues you didn't think about.

Microsoft, being who they are, could care less if you don't like the changes. They're going to make the changes, shove them down the

---

[74] Someone bought a new thesaurus!

market's throat and let God sort out the rest. For us mere mortals, we need to take some, not every, ideas into consideration.

If you're ready to make the change, find the "mouth" again. Win this person over first. Let the "mouth" work for you to spread the word about how fabulous the new change will be. Otherwise, the only change you will make will be changing your mind about the change.[75]

Understand that change takes time.

Don't expect the change to be instantaneous or accepted immediately. Sudden change can shake the confidence of the people it affects. No one likes to know it all one day, and be the "newbie" the next. Allow for the growing pains of change. Make sure people know that you expect them to change, just not overnight.

Anytime you hear an objection, you need to nip it in the bud right away. The longer you allow an objection to fester, the longer you'll need to win them over. If you let it go, the objector will think of more objections. They will build on the original objection. Address them right away; you don't have to solve them.

Answer objections immediately, if you can.

The longer it takes you to respond to an objection, the less credible your answer becomes to a person.

You need to have an answer at the ready. Before you talk to someone, you need to think about why someone would object to your idea.

List them all out. Even if they're not rational, you need to predict the possibilities.

---

[75] Can I use the word "change" a few more times in THAT sentence? Sheesh.

Do objectors stay rational for long? No.

They may start with a perfectly reasonable objection. If you answer that, they'll start thinking of crazy nonsense. You'll want to ask them "How did you get your job? People pay you to think like this?"

Sit down and think about why someone would dislike your idea. Get ready for the answers. Take the effort and time to plan objections out. Everyone wants their ideas to be immediately accepted. You need to be able to see the flaws in your own ideas. You need to accept people are going to say "no".

Never lie.

Often, when confronted with objections, if we don't have a proper answer at the ready, we'll make up a lie just to shut the objector up. Lies never work in the long term, and the longer the lie lasts, the more damage it usually ends up creating.

Listen.

Ignoring objections can be dangerous. Objections allow you to streamline, improve.

If you're going to complain and be an objector, you have to go about it the right way. You have to give them something in return.

You just took their idea, choked it, squeezed the life out of it and tossed it into the trash. You need to replace what you just took from them.

You can't just say, "That's a bad idea!"

Sorry, "That sucks!" isn't a good response to someone's new idea.

Even if it sucks stronger than a black hole.

If you do accidently forget to engage your filter and they ask "Why does it suck?"

"I don't know. It just sounds bad. Of all the things I've heard before, that idea sucks the most. And yet, I couldn't tell you why. It's like art. I know it when I see it and that idea sucks."

How useful is that kind of feedback? Does it really accomplish anything besides identifying you as a jerk?

When you do have a complaint and want to share it, you need to:

Explain why.

You can easily state you don't like the idea and then go through the laundry list of reasons you dislike the idea.

"I don't think that is the right approach because…"

Back up your own objections. They're going to defend their idea, you better take the effort to defend yours or you might as well keep quiet.

Being the "I told you so" person gets annoying.

Being the person who identifies the key problem and help improve it is seen as a "critical thinker".[76] If you have valid reasons why an idea is not good, you won't get dismissed out of hand.

Often a typical response to an objection is "Well, what's *your* idea?"

[76] I know its BS labeling to cover up negative thoughts that help us, but for this example, let's go with it.

Making a good idea on the spot is not easy. It takes planning and time. They sure took time thinking up their crappy idea. You probably need that time, too. Taking an honest look at why an idea may not work is still a valid way to be constructive.

If you can, give a replacement.

I said it's not always easy to think of an idea on the spot. Sometimes, things come to us in the moment. Offer your idea. "Why don't we try this instead?"

Don't be afraid to engage in a conversation or debate over ideas. A good manager or boss is always willing to hear constructive criticism and hear alternate ideas that will help the greater good. Especially if it is presented properly, in a non-threatening, non-accusatory ways.

Try to be nice when telling somebody their idea is total lunacy; don't be afraid to speak up.

If you are an employee, part your job is to protect the boss, just like their job is to protect you from making mistakes. If you see someone about to step on a landmine, don't you want to say "HEY! Don't take another step!"

Admittedly, there are people we would want to take that next step. In most cases, we try to help people avoid blowing themselves up. When your boss makes a mistake, it makes you look bad. If your employees make a mistake, it makes you look bad as well.

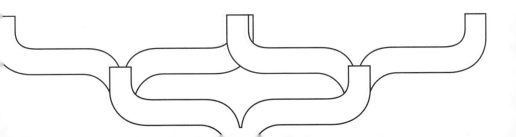

{ Make them spill their guts

If someone does have an objection, I like to use the "tip the bucket" method. You listen to the objection and when they are done, ask, "What other objections do you have?"

One of the weasely things objectors do is drip complaints like a leaky pipe. They'll only complain about one thing until it's addressed. Then, if it's resolved...BAM! They have another and another and another. They're saving the big one for last, too. They can drag out complaints that could have been resolved right away over a longer period of time.

This is often why people with legitimate complaints get disregarded. All because Sir *Bitch-a-lot* is their most common point of reference when it come to complaints. Which is why when they seem to be all done you ask, "Are you sure you have no other objections?" This way, you have some ammo if they come back in three weeks and start complaining about something else.

Think about the objection.

I know I said you need to answer immediately or lose credibility. But some objections you really need to think about. Especially if it is something you didn't plan for.

In a world of infinite complaints, you can't prepare for everything. I always assume I haven't thought of every possible contingency. I'm just not that smart. If you do not have an answer, let them know that they have a good point and that you'll need to think that over.

Maybe you'll realize they're not so wrong. We're looking for results, regardless of who comes up with them. You may have to put ego aside.

Handle the objection.

If possible, handle the objection.

If they complain "it costs too much," find somewhere you can cut something less important. If it's going to take too much time, look in to streamlining the process.

Once everything is completed, go back to the objector and follow up. They can tell you where problems are so you can improve the process. Plus they still feel involved, still feel part of the process and feel their opinions are valuable.

Sure, it's easier to simply yell "Back to hell, you vile bloodthirsty demon!" and a heck of a lot more fun. Sadly, it won't solve the problem.

Make it easier on yourself by simply listening to the problem; identifying the kernel of truth, recognizing that the complainer may have a valid point, or possibly even solving the issue.

You can exorcise the "undead" out of your life and concentrate on more important things.

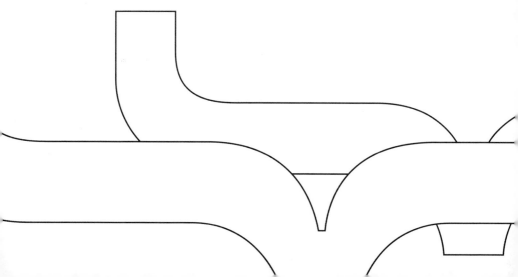

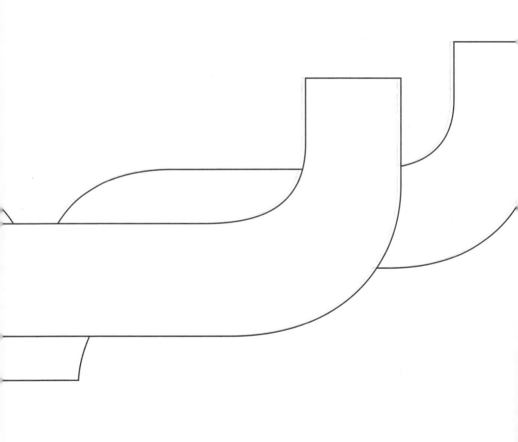

[Realist's Guidelines]
Complainers, Complaints and Objections

✴ Complainers are usually people with opposing viewpoints, who sincerely want you to avoid a mistake that could cause damage.

✴ Complainers won't stop until you drive a stake through their heart.[77]

✴ Reality Check: Don't disregard the message because you don't like the messenger.

✴ After you make a mistake:
  * Listen
  * Recognize
  * Solve

✴ Convert vampires so they are working for you.

✴ When dealing with objections:
  * Answer immediately, if you can
  * Never lie
  * When in doubt…pass the complainer on to the next sucker!

---

[77] My lawyers have advised me to make sure you understand that you don't literally drive a stake through their heart. That would kill them and make me an accessory. So don't kill anyone!!

FOR THE POSITIVE THINKERS:

Feel free to pass the buck, so to speak. Say you've got a complainer all up in your grill.[78] If the complainer starts griping too much, too often, simply agree with them. Then quickly leave them be for the next unsuspecting soul. "I agree! There is rarely enough creamy filling in an Oreo. I think you should write a sternly written letter!" Then disappear while they look for a pen.

Or sometimes you can aim them towards other complainers. If the two collide they might argue themselves out, complaining about who has it worse. All the while you are safely out of harm's way, doing what you do, enjoying all the things complainers seem to miss.

---

[78] I know how the hip-cats rap daddy-o.

CHAPTER 5:

Mumblings, Grumblings and Other Taboos

MOST OF US HAVE BEEN RAISED TO BELIEVE THAT WE SHOULDN'T SPREAD THINGS LIKE RUMORS AND LIES, WHICH I COMPLETELY AGREE WITH BY THE WAY. YET, WITH SO MANY PEOPLE TOLD NOT TO LIE, NOT TO SPREAD RUMORS, WHY IS THE INTERNET FULL OF THEM?

Why has the office water cooler become an oasis of water and seedy information?

Why are there more entertainment shows dedicated to who's dating whom than asking serious questions about politics, current events and world happenings? Even the "serious" news shows have more analysts spouting their opinion about facts than taking the time to actually talk about the facts themselves. They seem to thrive on rumors, lies and other shenanigans.

It seems, as much as we may personally dislike rumors and lies, that we're surrounded daily by others who practice such "dark arts."

Should we just ignore what's happening around us and go about our merry way? You can, but do so at your own peril![79]

Like all things that exist, even lies and rumors have some inherent value if you know how to handle them.

Like some volatile chemical, you need to tread lightly and carefully when dealing with lies and rumors or they too can blow up in your face. If you ignore them, they might just be the overlooked cause of your demise.

OBLIGATORY WORLD LEADER QUOTE:

"There are a terrible lot of lies going about the world and the worst of it is that half of them are true."

WINSTON CHURCHILL

---

[79] Not really…just overhyping a bit like the news does. See the Introduction. You read it, right?

{ Using rumors properly

We've all been there.

You're sitting with friends or at the company cafeteria with co-workers and someone tells you some real juicy gossip.

You weren't expecting it, you were just sitting there having a delightful chat and then it happens. "Did you hear…?"

Suddenly, due only to the company you keep, you're privy to a tidbit of info. What now?

{ **THE MYTH:** Rumors are ugly, horrible things.[80]

{ **THE REALITY:** Rumors can be a viable way to know what is happening around you.

How you handle rumors can be very important in how you are perceived and how quickly you can adapt to change.

Some rumors you need to know, others you need to forget as soon as you hear them. You need to process the rumor and be able to identify fact from fiction.

Never forget that credible does _not_ mean true.

I can say "Did you hear Steve is dating Julie?" I don't know who Steve and Julie are, but in any given situation, if both are single it could be a credible rumor that they might be dating.

Is it true? Now that's a completely different story.

---

[80] Only the good ones!

If I said Steve was abducted by aliens and he has a pod located in the basement of his house where they use mind control to take over the world, is that credible? Those of you without tinfoil hats would say no.

Credible means believable. Believable doesn't mean true!

{ Be a skeptical receptacle

I became a negative thinker, thanks to my dad. He's not a negative type person, he would just say some of the weirdest things.

His favorite was "I AM NOT YELLING!!" which of course he was.

Another one was "I am sorry, but I am not going to apologize." So let me get this straight, you're apologizing for not apologizing which makes that… you got it… an apology. The man is a genius.

Sometimes he would also make answers up just to see how we would react.

One time, when I was six or so, we drove to Florida. Somewhere near Georgia or so I saw these long strips on the side of the road. I asked my dad what they were.

They were strips of tires. My dad told me they were "alligator skins."

"See, an alligator's base core temperature is 78 degrees and when it gets hotter than that, it just peels a layer off and settles back into the swamp to cool off."

Okay. At 6 years old, at 60 miles an hour, you'll believe that.

This is the same man who told me yellow snow was lemon flavored.

Trust me, it's not even close.

When we finally made it to Florida, and we got to the hotel, he told me the light on the phone[81] was for deaf people.

"You see, when the phone rings, the light blinks and they know when to answer it."

What?!?

If they can't hear the phone ring, who are they talking to??

By doing this he did teach me, unintentionally I'm sure, a valuable lesson. Never take anything at face value.

Contrary to popular belief, it's okay to be skeptical.

I'm sure most Nigerian princes are wonderful people with generous hearts. Just not the one that emailed you yesterday.

You're not going to strike it rich stuffing envelopes in your spare time.

You can't win a lottery you didn't enter or even know about.

And you can't lose weight without dieting or exercise. As David Letterman once said "That just leaves disease, doesn't it?"

The old adage, "if it sounds too good to be true, it probably is," is a perfect example of skepticism and sound negative thinking.

Does that mean all opportunities should be avoided since they may be bad? Of course not! Remember, research is vital to any good business deal. If you don't do your due diligence, you're setting yourself up for disaster.

---

[81] The one that tells you "you have a message".

{ Rumor has it...

Rumors can be hurtful, incorrect and fun to talk about. All at the same time!

I suggest you try not to indulge your inner gossipmonger. It usually will only lead to trouble. Sooner or later, a rumor will land in your ear.

When you hear a rumor, use the three "L's":

Listen:

This is the fun part of the rumor process. Don't be afraid to listen to rumors. You want to know what's going on. Information is vital. Connecting to the grapevine can be invaluable. Now, if the rumor is personal and petty, it's useless to you. Just nod your head and never say a word about it again. Getting involved in personal rumors is how more problems can arise. Yet, you also want to know what's going on. A newsletter is not going to let you know what's going on. A specific memo is not going to give you the entire story. You'll pick up pieces here and there. Network the best you can.

 Listen to what they're actually saying. Is the BS meter going off in your head? That's always your first clue. If someone tells you something that you feel is just wrong, ask them to repeat it. Sometimes they hear their own delusional ideas and will change the information accordingly. People talk faster than they think, and giving them a chance to think things over allows them to get out the actual information they intended. It's always good to hear what information is floating around out there. You don't want to be on the outside looking in when something important goes down. At work, in your life, surprises can be fun or traumatic. If you can get hints or outright concrete evidence of something bad about to happen before it does, how helpful would that be?

Look up:

If something sounds iffy, doesn't quite jibe with you, look it up. Never take a rumor at face value. Verify. Go to the source, cut through the BS and find the truth by asking direct questions. Learn more about where they got their information. Sometimes the facts they heard are really rumors. When I hear the "uh…um…someone I know" without an actual name, I know it's BS.

Look up multiple sources, independent verification, all things journalists are supposed to do before going to print, you should do as well before you believe it. Don't fall into the trap of regurgitating rumors to the next person to find out the answers. Now you're the Bull spreading the BS. If and when the subject of the rumor finds out, your name may be the only one attached, regardless how far down the food chain you go.

Learn:

Water cooler talk can be valuable to you personally. You can identify resources in your company. Does Dave always seem to know what's going on before it happens? Does he tell you things that somehow always come true? He's a valuable resource, an information agent you can rely on. Martin, he says a lot of things, too. They always seem to be outrageous and never come to pass. Thanks to all the false

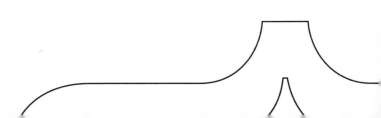

information, we now know Martin is an ignorant twit and to take anything he says with a grain of salt.

I can't tell you not to gossip at the office, because information is important in the workplace and you need to know what's going on behind the scenes. Rumors feed off speculation. The less you know about a rumor, the more it can spin wildly out of control and grow. It's okay to be skeptical as long as you are learning at the same time.

{ Damage control

One problem with rumors is what people don't know, they will make up. Since people naturally have a tendency to think negative thoughts, they are going to make the rumor much worse than the truth.

If something behind the scenes, like budget talks or layoffs, is going on they get blown out of proportion. If anyone merely speculates on something, it can be spread around like a virus, mutating into something out of control, regardless of the facts. Often a rumor that we hear is more interesting than the truth we know.

The longer a rumor lasts, the more damage it does. The longer you allow it to exist, the worse it will get. Morale will get down. People will blow things out of proportion, make stuff up, extrapolate some obscure unimportant fact into a monster that is totally untrue. They end up scaring themselves and other people.

TRY AVOIDING THESE PHRASES:

1. "Don't tell anyone I told you." That translates into "Hit the broadcast button. We're telling everyone!"

2. "This is just between us." Because as soon as they walk away, they'll tell someone else "this is just between us."

3. "Can you keep a secret?" The person asking that question obviously can't, since the next thing they will say is a secret they promised someone else they would keep.

Those three phrases, when you hear them, whatever comes out of their mouths, you know it will be juicy gossip, you know it will be interesting and you know it will be something you just have to tell someone else.

Avoid closed doors, especially when you know rumors are lurking about. If you know people are talking, closed-door meetings just end up breeding more rumors. When people feel excluded from information, it makes them suspicious. Their natural negative thinking kicks in and they'll assume bad things. Then they tell other people their suspicions, as often as possible. By holding closed-door meetings, you are telling the excluded there is something secretive[82] going on and they'll assume it's about them. That's human nature.

Try and have face-to-face conversations where questions can be asked and answered. When you can take the time to talk about what's happening, instead of piecemealing answers, much of the anxiety can be

[82] A.K.A. bad

set aside. Don't hide behind emails or memos, as they can be misinterpreted without an opportunity for clarification. People always read emails with a negative slant. Misinterpretations of a simple message can set back the entire process.

Rumors can get wildly out of control if we allow them to go unchecked. Knowing whom you can go to in order to get the *skinny* can be life saving. Don't spend your time rumor-mongering. Instead, identify reliable sources. It also verifies the wannabes who never have the right stuff.

{ Are your pants on fire?

Unlike complaints that have a kernel of truth to them, sometimes rumors can be bald face lies.

For example: "You look fantastic! Have you lost weight? You really should wear those pants more often."

Suspicious yet? You're probably wondering why I'm telling you all these things. Well, I'll be honest. I'm lying. You don't look fantastic. If you've lost weight, look behind you, you'll find it where your small butt used to be. And those pants don't make you look fat, your fat does. Too harsh? I'm sorry. Or am I?

{ **THE MYTH:** Lying is done by bad, evil people.

{ **THE REALITY:** Everyone lies.

Now before you think I approve of lying,[83] let's get real about lying. We all do it.

Ever say someone looked thin, when they didn't? Ever tell your wife "I would LOVE to go antiquing this Sunday. I didn't want to see the football game anyway"?

Lies are common occurrences and even if you're better than the rest of us and never lie,[84] people are going to lie to you. It's normal.

THERE ARE TWO TYPES OF LIES:

1. Lies to make us look better, like bragging and exaggerating, or to avoid making us look bad, like covering something up or lying by omission.

2. Lies that are used to spare someone else's feelings. These are the little white lies where the truth would be painful for the one who hears it and make us feel guilty if we actually said what we felt.

Lying is one of the negative things in life that happen. Some do it accidentally, some subconsciously, some vindictively. Sooner or later it's going to happen. The best way to figure out if someone if you suspect is lying to you is to:

---

[83] I don't...or do I??

[84] You're lying if you say you don't.

Ask direct questions.

By asking direct questions, you give the liar more and more rope to hang themselves with. As the old saying goes "You don't need to remember the truth." Asking a series of questions without getting the rubber hoses allows the truth to come out. In every cop drama they always ask the same question in various ways. They're looking for discrepancies. As soon as they can find an inconsistency, that's usually the thread they pull to unravel the entire story.[85]

Tell people you CAN handle the truth.

If people are lying to protect you or others, let them know you don't need the protection and would appreciate the truth even more than spared feelings. But you need to follow through with your claim. If you say you can handle something, you can't fly off the handle when they finally get enough courage to tell you the painful truth. You don't have to like the truth, or even accept the truth. You do need to react with some dignity. You don't want to be thought of as a liar, do you?

Don't be too judgmental.

If we know people lie, and we know that most people lie to protect others, we can't get too high and mighty when we catch someone lying. Odds are, you're going to get caught in a white lie yourself and I'm sure you'd appreciate a little understanding, too. Of course this all depends on the severity of the lie. It wouldn't be a white lie if it was something too drastic.

The best thing to do is not to lie at all. There's less work involved and less stress.

[85] It works on "Law & Order", so it must be true!

Would I lie to you?

Maybe. Then again…

{ The Blame Game

OBLIGATORY APHORIST QUOTE

"No snowflake in an avalanche ever feels responsible."

STANISLAW LEC

People say they don't want to play the "Blame Game," yet most people actively participate in it.

Blame, wrongly placed, is never good. The company can't seem to get the invoicing right, pricing is always screwed up and totals are incorrectly added up? Fire the mail guy. He's the one that allowed the invoice to leave the building!

Blame allows you to properly discover weaknesses and constant failings with a person.

If I'm working on a team and one person consistently is late, doing shoddy work, or not doing work at all, do I blame the entire team? I hope I wouldn't. I identify the weak link and either fix the issues or replace the team member.

The true problem with blame is that most people would rather place blame on other people instead of fixing the problem at hand. They spend precious time showing the deficiencies of another instead of showing their own strengths in overcoming issues. They would much rather set up a wall of excuses and blame to defend the arrows that inevitably will be aimed at them when this fiasco is over.

Different situations depend on how and when you deal with blame. Properly distributing blame at the right moment is a key ingredient in ongoing success.

Blame when the fire is out, not while the house is burning down. Standing around blaming people in the midst of a crisis is a poor allocation of resources.[86] You need to be putting water on the problem, not pissing on your people. Save what you can from a bad situation, rip victory from the jaws of defeat, dream the impossible dream… wait, now I'm quoting show tunes. Fix your problems first and then worry about what went wrong.

Sometimes you need to blame immediately, so you can take the matches away from the pyromaniac who consistently is playing with them. If Steve is consistently screwing everything up while you're trying to fix them, he needs to be eliminated.[87] He needs to be removed as part of the problem.

Then there are times you need to take one for the team. No one likes to be blamed. This is kind of the point. As a leader, we end up doing things we may not like to do, but it's what is best for everyone. Blame can be good in one aspect, it does identify the problem, yet if it causes stress and even more problems because of the stress, we as leaders need to jump on the blame grenade sometimes. Too many people helped in creating the problem, so blaming won't do anything but stir up resentment. Just suck it up, take the hit and let everyone move on.

[86] Wow. That sounded almost corporate!

[87] No, not by hired assassins. You watch too much "24."

{ Count on accountability – Leggo your ego

All this leads to the one of the most effective way of reducing all this lying, rumor mongering and blaming. By doing the one thing most people can't stand: being held accountable.

Yeah. I said it. You have to hold yourself responsible by practicing what you preach.[88] You have to be true to who you are and more importantly who you want to be.

Often, people who do a job feel they don't have to follow the same rules. They think either the rules don't apply or that they'll never get caught.[89] It's the side effect of too much self-esteem. There's a lack of humility that is becoming more widespread in our culture every day. People complain that today's youth have no sense of accountability. Where did they learn that from? From us!!

Look at how society is run. By all appearances, our judicial system seems to be geared toward the wealthy. If you have the money, honey, you get no time. Our kids grow up seeing this. If you have the money to get the dream team, you can buy your way out of trouble. Accountability is just one big check away.

Look at a few examples.

Former Buffalo Bills running back and Football Hall of Famer O.J. Simpson was acquitted for the murder of 2 people. It seemed to many that he got away with it. In fact, he promised to find the ac-

---

[88] Many televangelists and politicians just put down this book right now.

[89] I'm calling you out, Tiger Woods!

tual killers and for the past decade has scoured every golf course in Florida looking for them.

Actor Robert Blake was found not guilty for the murder of his wife. Admittedly, he did have the most outlandish alibi I've ever heard. Apparently, Blake told the police that he couldn't have possibly killed his wife because had gone back to the restaurant to get a gun he left at the table and that was when the shooting occurred! Again, the evidence seemed to be against Berretta, but an expert law team got him off.

Actor Mel Gibson was arrested for a DUI, made headlines for some nasty remarks about Jews and the incident disappeared after he went to some anti-Semitic rehab. What does that entail? 20 days in a synagogue and you come wearing a yarmulke and saying "shalom"? *Meshugenah Velt!*[90]

Regardless of these examples' true innocence or guilt, a pattern emerges. Rich people seem to get away with crimes that poor people couldn't. People quickly realize that certain people have different rules than the rest of us. This erodes accountability.

Society also is more about the person than the greater good.

Humility – [hyoo-mil-i-tee or, often, yoo-]

Noun – the quality or condition of being humble;
modest opinion or estimate of one's own importance, rank, etc.

[90] It means "It's a crazy world!" in Yiddish. If nothing else, you at least learned one new thing in this book!

I put the definition of humility here because from what I can see nowadays, no one knows what that word means. We've become a society of "look at me!" "I'm somebody!!" jerks. I know people who start conversations, not with "How are you?" "How's the family?" but with "Man, I've been so busy…blah…blah…blah." It's a way to make themselves sound important. They want to show people how valuable their time is. If it's so valuable and I'm talking to little insignificant you, you should feel honored!

We are a society looking inward and not outward. We're too worried about self-help that we can't be bothered with other people. I understand the philosophy of helping yourself so you can help others, like a crashing plane instructs passengers to put their air masks on before helping others, but we're helping ourselves without the thought of others. We're about self-promotion, not self-fulfillment.

There is a huge difference between self-esteem and pride. Self-esteem lets you know you're good at something, or you've done something worthy. Pride is letting other people know you're good at something, or you've done something worthy. A little self-promotion is certainly something we all do. We all like people to validate our abilities and accomplishments. It's human nature. Validating an accomplishment is not the same as accomplishing something for validation. One you did without expecting praise, the other you did for the praise.

Our egos are getting larger every day. As they grow in size, they get more sensitive as well. Humility makes your ego palatable to other people. Since we all have one, you might as make yours as digestible to others as possible. People like humble people, people want to be friends with humble people. People like to do business with humble

people. Nobody likes to write a check to an arrogant self-important jerk. I sure don't. How can we use negative thinking to be a little more humble?

You're not perfect!

Knowing this fact can be earth shattering for some and liberating for others. You make mistakes and bad choices all the time. You also make good choices, too. Understanding you're going to fall on your face now and again allows you to reduce the worry and stress of being perfect. The biggest problem in our lives is the stress we put on ourselves to be the best we can be. You can't be the best you can be every day. You can be pretty good most days, bad on a few and occasionally at your best. Do the math and you'll see you're usually doing pretty good or better most of the time. Being the best can be exhausting. There are times you have to be your best, so be prepared for those moments but don't use all your energy during warm-ups. Save your best for the game.

Don't keep up with the Joneses.

I don't know who the Joneses are. I do know their situation has nothing to do with yours. Screw the Joneses. Life is not a competition. Everyone's life and needs are unique. There may be a huge overlap of things in common, but just because the neighbor has a 72' LCD Widescreen 3D television with surround sound and a Blu-Ray player doesn't mean you need one.[91] Unless you want one for your Xbox. Then it's okay, as long as you're doing it because you want it, not because someone else has one.

[91] This technology became obsolete the moment I wrote it. This book is officially dated.

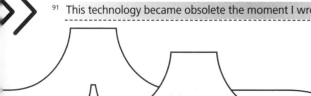

There are people who can do things you can't.

The opposite is true, too. So I can't hit a curveball and will never play with the Boston Red Sox. So what if I can't do complex calculations in my mind? Many athletes and mathematicians are horrible speakers.[92] I can do some things they can't. It's all relative, and yet one person's ability has nothing to do with another's inability. Appreciate others for what they can do and use their knowledge to learn from.

The biggest thing I can tell you about humility is just to treat people the way you want to be treated. Do you like being yelled at when you screw up? Then don't do it to someone else. I hear the word respect thrown out a lot. "I deserve respect" "Don't disrespect me." Are you showing the same respect you think you deserve? It's not someone else's responsibility to maintain respect for you. It's your responsibility to maintain that respect.

Accountability is like a subliminal message to the world. Instead of shouting from the rooftops, it slowly seeps into others. You act a consistent, reliable, trustworthy way, people will rely and trust you. If you spread rumors, lies or blame at will, the people around you will feel free to do the same.

---

[92] I've heard some of them. It's painful.

[Realist's Guidelines]
Mumblings, Grumblings and Other Taboos

* Credible does _not_ mean true.

* Yellow snow is _not_ lemon flavored!

* When dealing with rumors, use the 3 L's:
  * Listen
  * Look up
  * Learn

* "Don't tell anyone I told you" and "This is just between us" means they will tell everyone and anyone who will listen.

* Think you're being lied to?
  * Ask direct questions.
  * Tell people you CAN handle the truth.
  * Don't be too judgmental.
    Reality Check: Treat people the way you want to be treated.

FOR THE POSITIVE THINKERS:

Keep on the high road. If you steer clear of lies, rumors and the like, mud won't splatter on your nice white suit.[93] Or at least it won't splatter as much as if you were crawling around in it. Fingers in ears and yelling "LA-LA-LA!! I can't hear you!!" works as well. It will not only signal to people you do not wish to join in their reindeer games, it will also freak people out enough that they won't bother you in the future!

---

[93] Make sure not to wear it after Labor Day. That would be embarrassing.

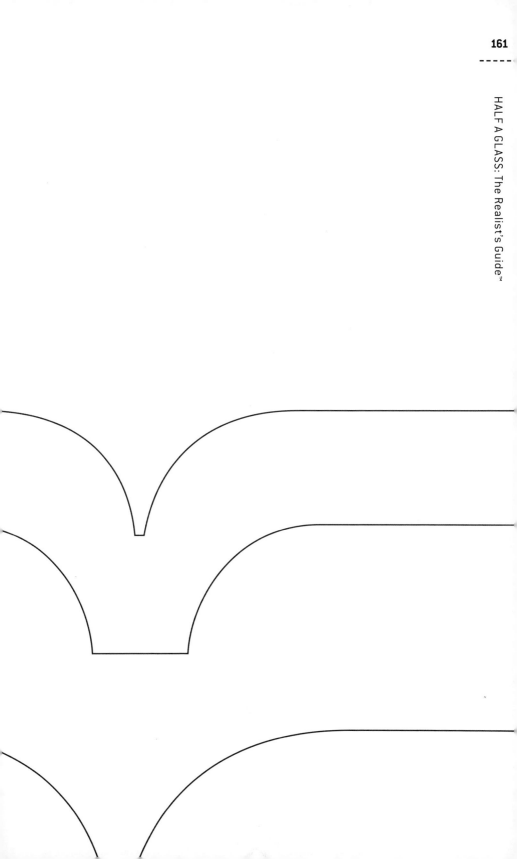

CHAPTER 6:

Goal Setting the Negative Way

WITH THE EXCEPTION OF THE INHERENTLY LAZY, MOST OF US WANT TO GET AHEAD. ACTUALLY, EVEN LAZY PEOPLE WILL WORK VERY HARD TO NOT HAVE TO WORK. THE POINT IS WE ALL HAVE THINGS WE WANT TO ACCOMPLISH, EVEN IF THAT'S TO ACCOMPLISH NOTHING.[94]

Some people want to reach the top of the mountain, others want to get past the tree line, while others just want to get off the flood plain. The problem is we don't always know how to get there. If we did, they wouldn't be goals, they'd be accomplishments. Goals allow us to start the planning stages of our successes.

If you never set goals for direction, how will you know where you're headed, how the trip is going or if you've arrived?

---

[94] You're doing great so far, keep it up!

THE MYTH: 3% of the world's population has written goals. They make most of the money and most of the decisions. They have the tools to move forward. If you don't have written goals, you're in control of those who do.

THE REALITY: While there is no proof of the 3% lording over the rest of us little people, writing things down helps us focus on what we truly want.

I hear many people say "I've got all my goals written up here in my head." Sure, that's a safe place. I have a tough time remembering where I parked at the mall, now I'm relying on my memory to guide my entire future??! Never mind the ADHD world we live in where our goals change from moment to moment, second to second. Our true long-term goals get lost in the immediate whims of the present.

Putting pencil to paper takes the fiction of your dreams and makes them fact. They bring your goals into reality, making them tangible. Many people avoid writing down their goals because they fear they will be chained to them. A constant reminder of the failure they think they are. "Here is written proof I can't accomplish what I want! " Remember, that's fatalistic thinking, not negative thinking. Negative thinking says "This is the goal I have and here are the obstacles I need to avoid."

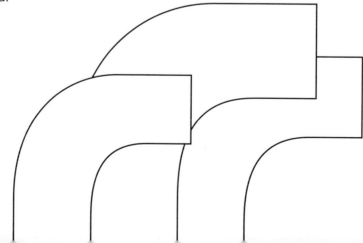

{ Goals

Why do you need goals, really?

When you set a goal it establishes a **direction**.

You always have a light at the end of the tunnel instead of just fumbling around in the dark. If you don't know where you're heading, how do you know you've arrived?

This is the easiest part, just think of something to do and WHAMMO! You've got a goal.

Need to find a new job? Goal.

Need to pay off your student loans? Goal.

Need to write a book? Goal.

Need to take a shower? Goal.

Need to win a soccer game? GOOOOOOOOOOOOOOOOOOAAAAAAA AAAAAALLLLLLLLLLLLL!

Anything and everything you want to accomplish, no matter how insignificant or profound is a goal. Sounds super productive, right?

Goals help identify expected **results**.

You can actually see progress or regression. You have tangible proof of success or failure. By knowing what is working or what is not, you can streamline your process, you can reach your goals faster.

Let's use finding a job as an example. You need a job that pays at least $50,000 a year with health insurance. As you interview and see the salary and benefits, you can make a more informed decision that allows you to reach your goal. You can tell by the offer if it's in line with what you want or need. Sounds simple, yet so often, people don't know what the end result should look like, so they have no idea if they're on the right track until they've wasted time, money and energy on the completely wrong thing!

Goals improve **teamwork**.

If everyone is on the same page, all focused on a common goal, they can eliminate duplicating work. They can cover more tasks by reducing redundancy.

Of course there will be overlap. It's necessary and unavoidable. As team members work together, they can combine their skills to be more efficient, spreading out the workload that in turn reduces stress for everyone.

Goals increase performance by setting **targets**.

People work harder when they can see the finish line. It's the carrot on the stick method. If the horse can see the carrot, it will move forward. If the carrot is two miles down the road, the horse isn't going anywhere. If that carrot is slowly moving forward, the horse will pick up speed, knowing that the carrot will soon be theirs.

Written goals allows you to **prioritize** more easily.

When you can visually see your goals, you can move them around. You can rank them by importance.

Write your goals on index cards and sit on the floor or place them on a table, whatever you need to do so you can see them all and easily adjust them.

If there are ever any goals that tie in importance, do the one that is the worst first. People have a tendency of pushing aside things they don't like to do, which actually draws the process out. By doing the hardest, most difficult priority first, you create momentum.

Goals must have certain attributes for them to be useful. Here is something you can use to make your dream into a goal.

{ D.R.E.A.M.[95] up some goals!

Since many people aspire to be rich, let's use that as the basis for creating our goal.

Duration

You have to set a time table for your goal. Is it going to take weeks, months, years? Without a time table, you never really have to do anything today. There's always tomorrow, right? Saying "I want to be rich by the time I'm fifty" is a real time table. I know that I have less than fifteen years to achieve this goal.[96]

---

[95] I was told to be any kind of successful "expert" I needed to come up with a catchy acronym.

[96] Plenty of time, right? *Gulp*

Realistic

Often we set goals well out of our reach. We need to bring our goals closer to our reach. I always hear that if you reach for the moon and miss, you'll land among the stars. Actually you'll fall to earth with a thud since the moon is actually closer than any star, unless you have an eternity to wait while you float aimlessly through space.[97]

"I want to be President of the United States" is an unrealistic goal. I'm not going to say it's impossible. Though, we've only had forty-four in the last two hundred thirty years or so years. That's only about five a generation. Five people out of the hundreds of millions of citizens. Pretty long odds, if you ask me. Being realistic is the hardest part for us, since we don't know what we can achieve until we're done achieving our goal. We can assume, we can hope, but know? Not until the deed is done.

We're going to try to set honest, achievable goals. When we meet them, we can expand to greater goals knowing we're able to progress. Remember, negative thinking doesn't always mean we can't. It just might mean we can't right now.

Exact

Your goal needs to be specific and straightforward. "I want to be rich" is not a specific goal. "I want to be rich by increasing my income through real estate investments" is. Being specific allows you to think of the goal in more tangible ways. You start preparing a plan. The more specific a goal, the easier it is to map out a strategy to obtain your goal.

---

[97] Ask anyone at NASA, They'll back me up.

Action-oriented

This is the how. How are you going to obtain your goal? "I want to be rich by finding a high paying job, saving money and investing properly" is action oriented. It's important to make sure every action is geared toward your goal. If making a lot of money is the goal, then every action must be a money generator. Wasting time on tasks that won't reach the final goal will only delay your success.

Measurable

They need to be a quantifiable goal. "I want to make 6 million dollars" is measurable. Make it something so precise you can calculate how close or how far you are from the end result. You can check at regular intervals and see if you are on pace or if you are behind and need to put more resources towards the goal.

{ Reverse engineering

So you have your DREAM goal. Now the big question:

Is what you are doing right now going to take you where you want to go?

We need to chart our path as best we can. Where do we start? By looking at the goal and working backwards. The best method to getting goals on paper is something I call "reverse engineering."

Start off with your dream, your vision, your goal. This is the title of your **"Master List."** This is what you want out of life. There are no limitations; it can be all cotton candy clouds and puppy dogs. The "sky's the limit" kind of goals. At this stage nothing is impossible. You want to win an Oscar, write it down. Take over the world, go for it. Don't let anything hold you back.

Then you move to **the 5-year plan**: Break down the steps you feel are necessary to obtain your goal on your "Master List." Which ones will take some time? Anything over a year, like "Get my Masters Degree," goes on this list. This makes your goals dreams with deadlines. Some may take longer than five years, but this is a good milestone to think about. Honestly, if you work on a goal, skill or practically anything for five years and do not see any substantial improvement, you're probably not going to get any better. It's okay to admit you suck at it. The past five years have proved that. Maybe you need different goals. Or maybe you need someone else to come in and help you.[98]

The 1-year plan:

This should be an attainable goal. Be realistic. It has to be something you can actually accomplish in the 365 days.

Then we move into the more obvious planning.

The Monthly plan:

What are you doing this month to reach the 1-year goals?

The Weekly plan:

What are you doing this week to reach your monthly goals?

[98] Outsourcing your dreams. I think I may have found the next big thing!

The Daily list:

What are you doing today to reach your weekly goals?

Maybe this timetable doesn't jive with your lifestyle. If you want, break it up into quarterly goals. If your goal is something like weight loss and you want to lose forty pounds this year, let's try and lose ten pounds a quarter. That just over three pounds a month, or less than a pound a week.

It will get tougher as we break it down into smaller chunks. If you do the work, you can see a realistic map to your goals. Don't be afraid to ask for help. Get others to brainstorm your plan with you. They will undoubtedly think of something you wouldn't have.

Feel free to write down your goals on the next page.[99] Think about one goal you have. It could be personal, like "I want to run a marathon" or professional, like "I want to become the VP of Operations." There is no wrong answer; they are your goals, after all.

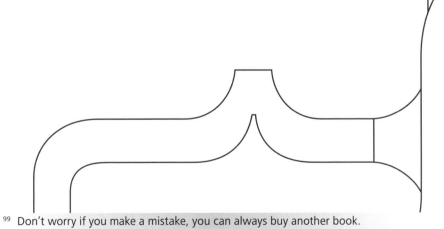

---

[99] Don't worry if you make a mistake, you can always buy another book.

Master List:

_____

_____

_____

_____

5-year plan:

_____

_____

_____

_____

1-year plan:

_____

_____

_____

_____

Monthly:

_____

_____

_____

_____

Weekly:

_____

_____

_____

_____

Daily:

_____

_____

_____

_____

Don't forget to ask yourself "why." Why do you want this goal? Think back to where I wanted to be Miss America. I couldn't, so I had to ask myself why I even wanted to be Miss America in the first place. If you forget the why, your goal is as meaningless, as if you never had one to begin with.

The last thing you do after you've written your goals down is to think about obstacles. Here's where negative thinking really helps.

OBLIGATORY OBJECTIVIST QUOTE

"The question isn't who is going to let me; it's who is going to stop me."

AYN RAND, THE FOUNTAINHEAD

What could stop you from obtaining your goals? What could go wrong and what would cause things to get off track? This is not an exercise to get you depressed and overwhelmed. It's an exercise to see potential problems and prepare for them so they don't surprise you. I call them problems, not setbacks. Setbacks slow you down. Problems, if prepared for, can be avoided and in the big picture can actually speed up the process precisely because you're not dealing with setbacks.

Look at what *might* happen and decide "Is there something I can do to avoid this issue?" If the answer is "no", ask "Is there something I can do to prepare me for this problem or at least lessen its impact?" Admitting that a goal has potential problems ahead is never a bad thing. Dwelling on them or using them as an excuse not to even make an attempt is a *huge* problem.

{ Get help – You don't have to fly solo

There is a widely held belief that if you want something done right, you and you alone must do it. This feeds into the romantic notion that one person can rise above the noise and build success with only their two bare hands. The idea is that we are lone travelers, overcoming obstacles with only our own wits and willpower. To this I say... what a waste of effort and time. I don't know about you, but I'm getting some help!

No one becomes a success without help. No one.

Think about all the successes you know in your life. Then look at the support system in place that assisted in that success. It may not be obvious for some, yet they all got help somewhere, somehow. A great basketball player like Michael Jordan didn't win championships until Scottie Pippen, Dennis Rodman and Horace Grant showed up. You should get help, too.

Negative thinking says you can't do everything. It doesn't say you can't do anything; rather, it focuses a bit of reality on every situation. Learning to ask for help is one of the biggest steps towards achieving your goals you can take.

How do you ask for help?

It's not something we do readily, admitting our deficiencies. If you can get past that ego driven nonsense and look at what your needs really are, asking for help can be very easy.

Ask others if they need help.

You have to give to get. The old saying "you have to spend money to make money" works with help, too. You need to be helpful if you want people to return the favor. Ask people if you can help them. Be sure that the help you offer is something you can help with; otherwise, you could just compound the problem. If you can't help that person, refer them to someone who can. Ironically enough, that alone is very helpful!

Be clear on what you need.

This is the tricky part. You need to explain to the person willing to help exactly what you need. Even if you don't know what you need, at least tell them the outcome you want. By clearly defining your outcomes, they can get to the heart of the matter, saving time and frustration. Sometimes, explaining what you are doing now will allow your helper to see the problems that are obstructing your path to success. It's just like the plumber asking what you put in the disposal that caused the clog. This way he knows which tools he needs to fix it.

Be grateful.

I can't say this enough. If someone goes out of their way to help, be thankful. Show your gratitude. People are more apt to help you again if you reward them with sincere "thank you" or show of appreciation.

Asking for help is not a weakness. It is the sign of a person who is confident, understands what needs to be done, and yet also understands their own limitations. It shows you value other's opinions and expertise. It also shows that you know how to get things done...even if you're not the one who knows how to get those things done yourself.

It's a tough and sometimes unforgiving world out there. Trying to stubbornly plow ahead on your own isn't a sign of strength. It's not a sign of superior intellect. It's just plain ego. Ego is not a bad thing, but if you're going to sabotage yourself simply because you are trying to be the person with "the answer", that tough world is going to get a lot tougher. However, if you're willing to ask for and accept help, the world isn't much of a problem at all.

Now that you have your goals written down somewhere, please don't throw them in a drawer, never to be seen again. Put it somewhere you have immediate access to. Check your goals often to see how you are doing. Most importantly, adjust your goals as you move forward. Constantly change and adapt your goals to your progress. If your goals are easily obtainable, you'll get bored. If they're out of this world, you'll give up. See where you are. Are you progressing? Is the progress fast or slow? Too fast, push the goal further way. Too slow, readjust your definition of success so you just might make it to the finish line. As you work on them, you will discover various answers to achieving your goal you didn't think of while you were writing them. As these little nuggets land your field of view, add them to your goal sheet. Cross off goals when you accomplish them. Do whatever you need to so you can measure success and failure.

The last thing you need to do is put these goals somewhere where you'll see them. You'll be reminded of them, encouraged by them, maybe shamed by them as well…whatever it takes for you to act on them! Put them on a wall calendar, a white board in your office, or maybe just some sticky notes around your monitor. Put them somewhere where they're in front of your face. Out of sight means out of mind! Don't put things in the black hole of your desk drawers.

{ I can't get no satisfaction!

You've written your goals down. You've gained some insight and direction. Maybe you even have accomplished a goal or two.[100] Somehow the overwhelming happiness and feeling of satisfaction either didn't come or didn't quite last as long as you'd like. You may even be thinking "What gives?! Why am I still working so hard? Why am I not satisfied with what I've got?"

Not to worry. That is totally natural. It's part of the human condition to want more, do more, and become more. Idleness is not only the devil's workshop, it's bad for your brain and not very good for society.

What if we just gave up after we discovered fire?

"You know, we're warm, we can cook our food and the light scares away animals. I'm good."

[100] You're welcome!

We'd still be living in caves. We moved out of caves because we got sick of cold, wet rock. We built the wheel because we got tired of lugging all our crap with our hands. We invented writing because somewhere, someone forgot something and another person said "Sheesh. I wish there was a way of remembering all this stuff!"

We get promoted, master our job and then start looking around to see how we could fit into our supervisor's place. Humans are conditioned to never be satisfied. You'll have moments, possibly extended moments of contentedness. Soon enough, you'll get antsy for more.

It's why retirees find post career jobs; it's why we have hobbies. It's why my wife wants to remodel our home every few years. Boredom! Our brains must always be occupied with something or we go crazy.

Ambition can be destructive if we let it overwhelm us, if we allow it to make us cutthroat mercenaries with only our best interests in mind and we don't care how we achieve our goals as long as we do. This can alienate people and actually slow progress. Too often people undermine others, disregard people in the pursuit of their own happiness, which turns people off, which in turn makes people unhappy. All that work and effort to be happy is wasted, since we have no one to share it with because we drove them all off with our assholiness.[101]

Wanting more, wanting a better lot in life is the human condition. Try not to get too upset with yourself because you're not completely satisfied. You never will be. It's the constant craving of evolution.

With all these goals outlined and written down, you'll start to make a

---

[101] Sounds like a religious leader doesn't? Ladies and Gentleman, please rise for his Assholiness.

road map to go where you want. I can't guarantee you'll make it to the Promised Land, but at least you can aim your nose in the right direction.

If you are one of those inherently lazy people with little or no ambition: Congratulations! You made it to the end of the chapter! Now go brush off those potato chip crumbs and find a job. You're taking up valuable basement space that your parents would love to use as storage.

[Realist's Guidelines]
Goal Setting the Negative Way

✳ Writing things down helps us focus on what we truly want.

✳ If there are goals that tie in importance, do the one that is the most difficult first.

✳ D.R.E.A.M. up some goals!
  * **D**uration
  * **R**ealistic
  * **E**xact
  * **A**ction-oriented
  * **M**easurable

✳ Reverse engineering
  * Master List
  * 5-year plan
  * 1-year plan
  * Monthly
  * Weekly
  * Daily

✳ Ask yourself "Why?"

✳ Reality Check: No one becomes a success without help. No one.

FOR THE POSITIVE THINKERS:

Dream as big as you can! Not everyone can grow up to be president. Maybe you're one of those who can. Map out your wildest dreams, find like minded people to emulate and get advice from. Someone has to beat the odds; otherwise, it wouldn't be called gambling. It would just be called losing!

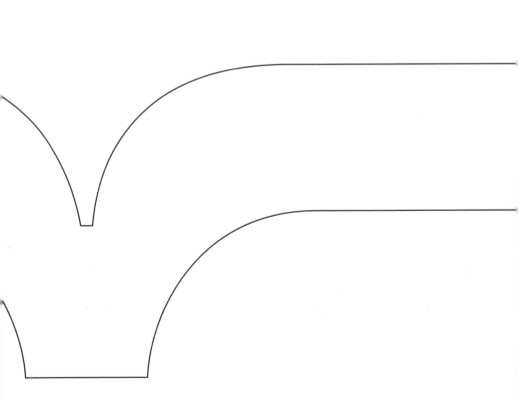

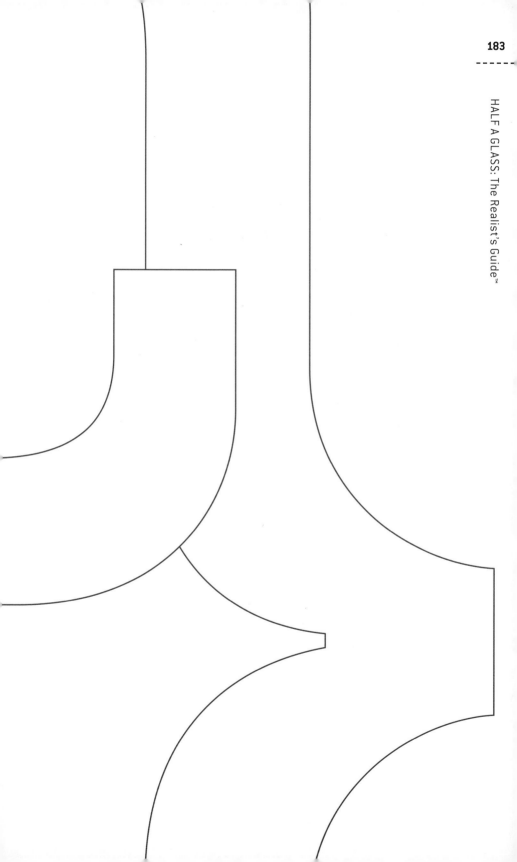

CHAPTER 7:

Not So Great Expectations

You've learned about your attitude. I just told you how to set goals

and you're ready to take on the world! You've got your head in the clouds, ready to reach for the moon! I say, slow down there big fel-la.[102] Not so fast. Are your expectations out of whack? Most likely. Often we aim so high and make so many, we can't possibly succeed.

By idealizing our goals, putting them on pedestals, visualizing unreal outcomes, we crash pretty hard when the reality slaps us in the face. That fall can cause major depression. The yo-yo of expectations can make the mood swings that much worse. There's an old sports cliché that say "Don't let your highs get too high and your lows too low." Think of it as a sign that says "You must be at least this crazy to get on this ride." Avoid the cruel roller coaster of emotions if you can.

---

[102] Or little lady…I find most ladies do not like to be referred to as Big Lady so if that's sexist, so be it. At least I'm not getting by butt kicked by a heavy set woman.

Not that we should be a society of emotionless robots. Managing your expectations, managing your emotions due to expectations can really take the stress and burden off many people. It may actually allow you to enjoy your life on a more consistent basis. Imagine that!

I'm not saying you can't have high placed goals. You just need to have realistic expectations. People confuse them as the same. My goal is to be a millionaire. My expectation is that's not going to happen overnight. Not without a Lotto ticket, anyway.

Expectations can be helpful motivators or a crushing weight around our necks, choking the joy and very life from us, like that ugly sweater that's two sizes too small.[103] By lowering expectations, you can actually breathe easier, allowing yourself to achieve your goals without all the stress.

Lowering expectations isn't a bad thing. I'm sure the divorce rate would be lower if everyone lowered their expectations. I think people are looking for that perfect person. Well, I hate to break it to you. That person doesn't exist. They snore, they forget your birthday, or they put clothes "on" the hamper instead of "in" the hamper. They sing off tune, or they sing songs and replace the actual lyrics with dirty lyrics.[104]

Every person in the world does something that irritates you. It may be something very minor and despite their "Star Wars" collection, you love them anyway. Sometimes it's something major, like not knowing that hitting on your sister is a bad thing. No one is that perfect prince or princess you are hoping for. There are a lot of compatible people

---

[103] Yes, I've seen it. You should probably burn it just to be safe.

[104] My wife's biggest peeve.

out there that with effort[105] can be a very happy and productive life.

You may want to be the richest man in the world. Yet, once you realize you don't need billions of dollars to be okay, things become more enjoyable. Stress is reduced and you can go about living the life you have, instead of the one you were "supposed to do."

Trying to hit a homerun every time out will cause more strikeouts that hits. Take a good honest swing at it, though. You can't be perfect every time. Many tasks do not even require perfection. They require completion. If you look at expectations as "Best Case Scenarios" instead of the only acceptable outcome, you'll realize that less than perfect can still be pretty damn good.

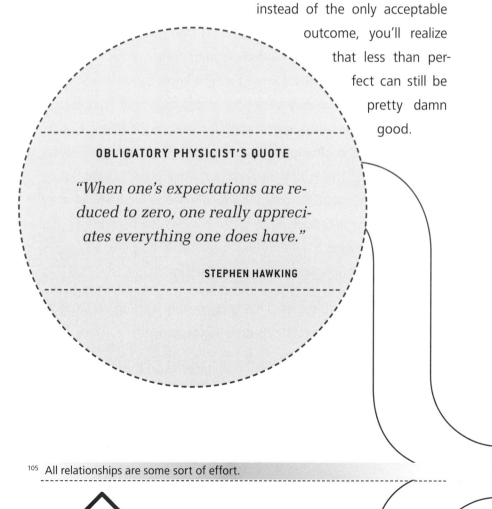

OBLIGATORY PHYSICIST'S QUOTE

"When one's expectations are reduced to zero, one really appreciates everything one does have."

STEPHEN HAWKING

---

[105] All relationships are some sort of effort.

{ Where do expectations come from?

You're not going to like the answer. I'm not here to tell you want you want I'm here to tell you what you need. Most expectations are put on us...by ourselves![106] We can blame our parents, our society and culture,[107] but the biggest source of expectations comes from within. Since we are naturally negative people, we usually put the hardest and least realistic expectations squarely on ourselves.

Why? Most often it is because we crave approval from others. Usually from people we may never get approval from. Some people crave approval from people they have never met, never will meet or don't really want to meet, yet we want them to know how awesome we really are. Like the snobby neighbors across the street who recycle everything, like somehow global warming really is their fault. Not humans in general, but them specifically, and they are trying to recycle their guilt away! This is why they put that huge green bucket out by the street. Sure, while it's green to identify recyclable material, they revel in the fact they have more green buckets than anyone on the block, thus showing the world how responsible they are. All I see is people who consume and create more garbage than I do.

We want everyone to see us in the best possible light, so we struggle with our own high expectations to feel accepted.

Other people place expectations on themselves so they can be used

[106] Didn't expect that answer, did you?

[107] Which I will in a moment.

as guidelines, mile markers. They get a great sense of achievement when they meet these expectations and it drives them. This can be a very good way of motivating yourself, pushing yourself for bigger and better things. Taken too far it can create a sense of hopelessness and inadequacy. Then again, your situation may be hopeless. Sadly, you may be inadequate. Feeling warm and fuzzy yet?

Coming in a close second, and possibly the reason you allow yourself to put expectations on everything you do, is your friends and family. When I say friends and family, I really mean your family. These are the people who have raised you, taught you right from wrong and how to behave in public.[108] In theory they gave you all the tools you needed to be part of society.

They put expectations on who you should date, what kind of job you should have and what success should look like (in their eyes, anyway). They do this out of love. Misguided, irritatingly inappropriate, guilt riddled love, but love nonetheless. They only want what they think is best for you. They want you to study hard so you get into a good school, so you become a doctor or lawyer so you can provide for the family you may have some day. You just want to smoke pot and go to college to meet girls. Since they're the ones paying for it, they want results. Results so they can stop paying for you and you can pay for yourself.[109]

Other family members are just looking out for you and assume their experiences will translate into ways you can be successful. Times and culture change. I can't imagine my parents giving me advice about

---

[108] Your car is technically in public, so don't pick your nose there. I can see you!

[109] Am I getting a bit too personal?

kids sexting[110] or putting inappropriate pictures on Facebook.[111]

They raised their kids without the internet; they didn't have television shows dedicated to warning about internet predators. My parents gave me a key and a phone number, told me to walk to and from school by myself and I was only allowed one phone call in the afternoon. That was to my mother so she knew I was home. Not because she was worried I might get kidnapped, but to make sure I didn't go off somewhere I shouldn't be getting into who-knows-what kind of trouble. Some advice is universal, yet each generation has new challenges and experiences that older generations never faced before.

Some family members want to live vicariously through their children. The kids are seen as a clean slate, to be everything they were not, to fulfill all the dreams they couldn't. You see this with dads and kids who play sports. The kids want to play, have fun, run around. Dad wants to WIN! They will argue with every call regardless of how embarrassing it may be. Lately there have been parents willing to fight and even kill people over youth sports. Talk about putting too high an expectation on a kid!

> **I WAS LUCKY, THE ONLY THING MY PARENTS EXPECTED FROM ME AND MY BROTHER WAS:**
>
> 1. Don't become a drug addict.
>
> 2. Don't go to jail.
>
> 3. Be a somewhat productive member of society.

---

[110] Texting sexual messages for you old fogies or are you so old I need to explain texting?

[111] Or as my parents alternately call it BookFace and FaceMate. Old people are so cute!

I think they beat all expectations. Good work!

Society also puts expectations on us. The media and advertisers pressure us to buy or behave certain ways. Drink certain things, drive certain cars. Often these types of expectations are exaggerated to the extreme. Models that are wafer thin, with perfect airbrushed skin and the proper bone structure. No one tells the public that the pictures were so drastically altered that you probably wouldn't recognize the model if you tripped over her in drug rehab. This constant barrage of unrealistic expectations trains our mind to put undue pressure on ourselves.

Your workplace puts expectations on you. Not just your manager, but the entire organization sets goals and targets out of your control. Sales quotas, productivity measurements, policies and procedures that outline what they expect from you. Dress codes and time cards. When to take lunch breaks and for how long. What can be expensed and what cannot.[112] Show up to work sober and on time? Not for the salary you're paying me, pal! Now let me get back to my two hour lunch, you're harshing my buzz, dude.

{ What did you expect?

Don't think you're innocent from putting expectations on others. We put small and large expectations on everything and everyone. You like your pizza a certain way, you know how much a new Toyota Camry should cost, or you tip a waiter based on certain conditions you place on them.

---

[112] Who knew that a lap dance wasn't expensable?

We expect long lines at the post office every April 15th, a three day weekend for Memorial Day, and we expect lawyers and car salesmen are out to screw us. Right or wrong, we expect things all the time.

When you get married, you expect that person to love, honor and obey. Well, maybe not obey, but at least pretend that they might do something you ask them to every now and then. Wives expect men to put the seat down after they are done, men expect women to look before they sit their bare bottom somewhere. Expectations to help support the family unit, to attend certain family function, to fulfill obligations.

You want your kids to do well, be smart and creative. Apparently those kids are never the ones sitting near my table whenever I go out to eat. I've learned to expect that.

You expect that if you work hard, you will be rewarded. Not always the case, yet not an unrealistic expectation. You expect to make more money as you get older, gain more responsibility, and get more power as you move up the ladder.

Heck, I bet you were expecting this book to be a lot better or worse than it is. Maybe you were expecting a miracle method that would save your life and make you a whole new you.[113] Maybe you never expected you'd read this much of it, yet here you are.

With all that expecting going on, I'm not about to tell you to stop making expectations. You can't and I don't expect you to. You can take a look at your expectations and see if they're causing more harm than good.

[113] If that were true I'd have charged more!

{ Managing expectations

As we set goals and expectations, we need to sprinkle a dash of negative thinking so we can cope with failure and also plan for success.

Look at your expectations.

Are they realistic? Are they grounded in reality or some dream world where everything happens perfectly to maximize your happiness? Wild and unrealistic expectations will always lead to disappointment. Make sure your dreams and goals are just out of reach so you can push yourself to improve and occasionally reach beyond your grasp. Just not so far away that failure is the only real option. Take an honest assessment of your abilities and inabilities. If you have to, write them down, both the skill you have and the skills you need to achieve. Hopefully there will be lots of similar skills on both lists. Focus on the ones missing on your skill list. Can you find a way to obtain the skill, either on your own or from someone else? Very rarely do you need to rely 100% on you and you alone. You can get help. Very few people succeeded on their own. There was a support system in place to compensate for any deficiencies.

Have several strategies.

Since you really don't know which plan will succeed, it's good to have more than one plan in case something happens to slow your progress. Often people fall in love with one idea, no matter how difficult, inaccurate or downright ridiculous they may be. Without a backup plan, what do you do if things go wrong? Become severely disappointed, that's what. Having multiple options allows you to spread your expectations around. All your proverbial eggs are not in any one basket.

Ask yourself:
"What would I suggest to a friend in this situation?"

It's comical how much better we are at doling out advice to others than using that same advice for ourselves. We can routinely tell people how to live their lives, run their businesses, and fix their relationships. When it comes to living our own lives, whoo-boy! We outright suck. We can't filter out our own expectations. We have none for the person we are telling. We just give them the information we feel is the most helpful regardless of the perceived outcome. Think about things as if you were talking to somebody else. For a few of you, you are doing that right now.[114] For the rest of us, it takes a concerted effort. Take the time to think about your issues as if you were not emotionally invested. You'll be surprised how good, logical, reasonable and clear your answers might be.

Don't over promise.

A good way to manage the expectations of others is not to guarantee perfection. We often get ourselves in trouble by telling people we can do more; perform faster, with greater results than we can deliver. Sometimes this pushes us to overachieve. Often it gets us in trouble and causes far more stress than we need. By lowering the bar, you can often jump right over it, making everyone happy. Take Scotty, the engineer of the starship Enterprise, from Star Trek.

NERD ALERT!
The following example is nerd-centric. Proceed with caution.

---

[114] I hope the new prescription helps out.

He always told the captain it would take more time to fix something than it really did. Why? For one, if there was something unusual in the fix, he had a buffer of time. His real reason? When he completed the task early, he looked like a miracle worker!

Face your Expector.

If someone is putting expectations on you that you feel are unrealistic or unnecessary, talk to them about it. Sit them down and discuss why they have these wild expectations. Ask them how they came to expect all this. Be nice about it, though.

Try <u>not</u> to say the following:

Are you high?

Did you fall on your head?

Who the hell do you think you are?

You're out of your freaking mind!

Are you just stupid?

You're as bright as a dark room with the door closed.

Let's talk about this…right after you pull your head out of your ass.

Instead, try saying:

I appreciate your confidence in me.

This is a pretty ambitious project.

Let's talk about what we can do and what we can't do.

How do you see this happening?

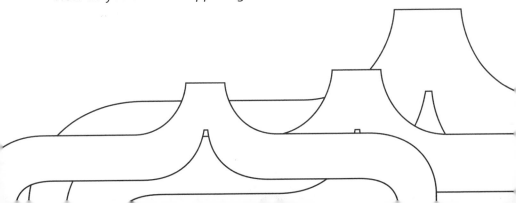

Talking things out in an honest manner builds trust, rapport and eases the burden. Maybe the expector doesn't understand what is needed for their expectations to be realized. When I worked in tech support long ago, people thought Star Trek and the Matrix were real examples of where technology was in the real world. If they can scan someone in 2 seconds, how come it takes 4 hours to download a file?[115]

Your expector may not realize the undue stress they are placing on you. Even if they know you can meet their expectations, applying stress and pressure may reduce your ability to achieve. This is why you must:

RELAX!

Harder than it looks, stressing out over expectations can be both helpful and hurtful. Stress by its very nature can cause health problems, distractions and general grumpiness. Stress also prepares us by letting us know where weaknesses might be. Try and bring your stress down to a level where it allows you to be aware of potential problems, but not so much out of control that we're getting ulcers.

OBLIGATORY OLD-FOGEY
ROCK BAND LYRIC

"You can't always get what you want..."

THE ROLLING STONES.

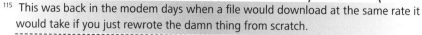

[115] This was back in the modem days when a file would download at the same rate it would take if you just rewrote the damn thing from scratch.

{ Dealing with disappointment

Disappointment is a regular occurrence for many people. It happens to everyone. You're expectations take control and you think something good is going to happen and WHAMMO! It doesn't. Or it does, yet it's not nearly as good as you thought it would be. Kind of like any Harrison Ford movie in the past 15 years.

You know Harrison Ford, you like Harrison Ford; he had a great track record for the 1980's and early 90's. Then he started making crap like *Six Days, Seven Nights*, *Random Hearts* or worse, *Hollywood Homicide*. And you fall for it every time he makes a movie because you remember all the good stuff he made. Maybe every couple of years he sneaks in an acceptable film, like *What Lies Beneath* or the barely passable but not horrible *Firewall*. Basically, while it's mediocre crap, you want to believe.

We do the same thing with people and experiences. I was always told, especially in high school, "Enjoy this time, they'll be the best years of your life." I always thought "Really? This is the best? It gets worse from here? Wow…"

Thankfully, that was a big huge lie, told to me by bitter older people whose own lives turned to crap. I've found life gets better as you get older. At least for me it has.

Any time another person is responsible for your own happiness, you'll most likely be disappointed. You can't control other people so why put expectations on them? You can hope they do what you'd like. Wish them well and give them advice. Other people can only disappoint you if you put expectations on them. Doing that takes you out of the driver seat and now other people control your outcomes and responses. Sounds like a bad deal, if you ask me.

You may need to make compromises. Don't fall into the trap of "wanting it all." You'll always be disappointed. Try for some at first. Then, down the road, try for more. Then, when you really have all cylinders firing, try for as much as you can get. But "all"? All is perfection and that can never be obtained. Besides, perfect is boring. Imperfection can be so much more fun!

When disappointment happens, understand that it is not the end of the world. You may have missed out on an opportunity this time. Don't worry. Another will come along. The next time you'll have the knowledge of the previous failure to help guide you, unless it's the actual end of the world. Then we're all screwed, so realize you're in the same boat as the rest of the planet and we are all disappointed.

You can aspire to be something better, just don't expect it to happen.

You can hope to improve, just don't get too disappointed if it doesn't.

OBLIGATORY CONTINUATION-OF-ANOTHER-QUOTE QUOTE

"...but if you try real hard. You get what you need."

THE ROLLING STONES.

Maintaining your positive attitude while tempering it with some healthy negative thinking will allow you to be happier in the long run without sacrificing your dreams to do so.

I would expect nothing less!

[Realist's Guidelines]
Not So Great Expectations

✱ Reality Check: Every person in the world does something that irritates you.

✱ Most tasks do not require perfection. They require completion.

✱ Expectations are put on us by:
  * Ourselves
  * Our friends and family
  * Society
  * Work

✱ We put expectations on others, just like they put them on us.

✱ Manage expectations by:
  * Keeping them realistic and just out of reach. Too far, we get frustrated; too close, we get bored
  * Have several strategies
  * Don't over promise
  * Face your Expector – Let them understand the pressure and stress being put on you.
  * Relax

✱ Harrison Ford hasn't made many good movies in 15 years.[116]

✱ You can't control other people, so don't put expectations on them.

---

[116] Sorry, it had to be said!

FOR THE POSITIVE THINKERS:

Load 'em up! If you feel you can do anything, go for it. Surprise yourself. Astound others. Don't set limits if they are going to limit your ability. Go above and beyond as often as you can.

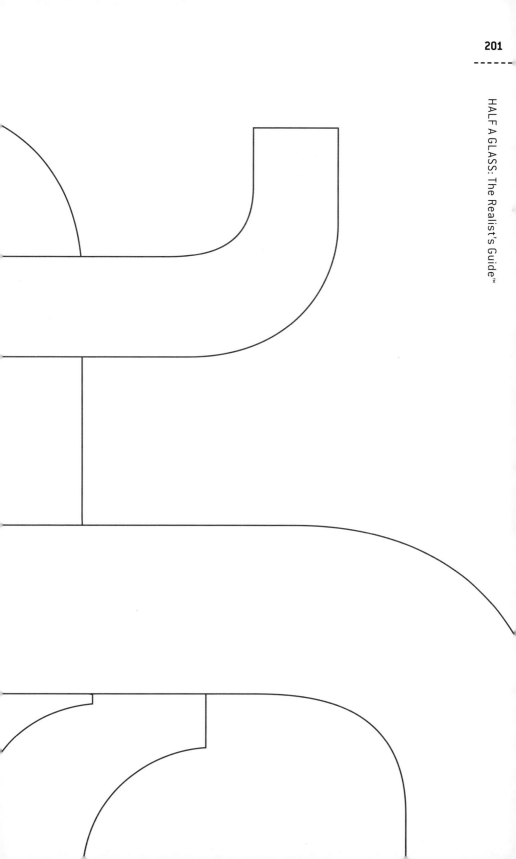

CHAPTER 8:

The Power of Negative Thinking

It's the last chapter.

For those of you who cheated and skipped to the end, you're probably looking for the part where I tell you to walk on fire or hunker down in some sweat lodge. Neither would I suggest to you.

Walking on fire sounds amazing! In reality, it's a trick to falsely build up your self esteem.

Why would I make you do that?

Feet smell bad enough. Just imagine the reek of them burnt!

And sweat lodge?

Hello?!

The word *sweat* is the first and only thing I need to hear before I say in my best Whitney Houston voice "Hells to the no!"

There is nothing worse than a room full of overly positive sweaty people with burnt feet. You can't Febreze a memory like that away.

Where are the affirmations?[117]

Where are the heartfelt stories of unbelievable anecdotes used in place of real facts?[118]

Where are the contrived analogies?

Here, try this:

I don't see negativity as a road you travel down. Roads are placed by people. We can put roads anywhere we want leading to anywhere we like.

Negativity is more like a river.

It can be raging rapids of overwhelming power or just a small stream, but it's always there, naturally.

Like rivers, we can harness that power; use its natural force for our own productivity.

Our dam is our decisions on how we are going to use the river.

Some dams just stop up the river completely by trying to shut it out, but at some point the rising water behind the dam will go beyond our control. Others, like myself, can open our floodgates, control the flow and use it to generate electricity.

Trying to eliminate negativity is like trying to stop a leaking dike.

[117] Not going to happen.

[118] Please. By now you should know what the deal is.

You put your finger in a hole, another leak will happen somewhere else. Stop trying to fight the rushing water and find a way to utilize the power created.

Done rolling your eyes yet?

Want real motivation? Want to really be inspired whenever you're taking on a task? Make informed decisions. Take the time to think things through so you make the right decision. It's not as hard as people make it out to be.

OBLIGATORY DEMOTIVATIONAL QUOTE

"If a pretty poster and a cute saying are all it takes to motivate you, you probably have a very easy job. The kind robots will be doing soon."

DESPAIR.COM

{ Is being reasonable so unreasonable?

Have you ever had a bad boss?

The kind you wonder, "How the hell did this guy get to run this company?"

They're arrogant, temperamental, sarcastic, insensitive and borderline incompetent. Yet somehow there they are, running the show.

Don't get me wrong, there are a lot of great bosses out there. Wonderful, caring, down-to-earth folks who get that their biggest and best asset are their people.

Just as many jerks and idiots are in charge as well, proving that personality is not always the key. If you work hard, stay focused and make the right decisions, you can succeed.

Not all negative thinkers are obnoxious punks.

Just the ones we remember. It wasn't the negativity we remembered, it was their assholiness[119] so we start to associate anything "off-putting" as negativity.

A mom's worry is negative thinking.

The stewardess's preflight safety talk is negative thinking.

The virtual labyrinth of customer service security questions when all you want is your bank statement is negative thinking.

We need to separate the process of negative thinking with the stereotype of curmudgeonly bastards.

Negative thinking isn't a philosophy; it's a tool that fits into your existing attitude.

You can be cautiously optimistic and realistically hopeful.

Positive attitudes and negative thoughts can coexist without your head exploding!

---

[119] There it is again!

{ Lights. Camera. Action!

Now that you've seen the light, how can we turn this new knowledge into action? Good question![120]

Let's get negative!

Don't let doubts and fears stop you.

Allow them to let you catch your breath. Understand where they come from, why they're bubbling to the surface. They're mental warning signs that often are there to protect you from harm. You can choose to ignore them…after some consideration.

Our hopes and dreams excite us into action, push us in a direction, and fuel our drive. They're the lifeblood of humanity and we certainly wouldn't be here in the 21st century, living as well as we have been, without them. Negative thinking doesn't stop us from achieving. It helps map out our strategy to achieve.

Flex your muscles.

You want to be buff, toned, ripped or any other term used to describe a muscle-bound He-Man/She-Ra?[121] We have to know what are our strengths are, keep them honed and ready at the drop of a hat. We also need to recognize our weakness so they don't lock the door of opportunity we're trying to kick in with our strengths.

Start listing out what you can and cannot do. Then honestly assess if

---

[120] I'm glad I asked that totally spontaneous unplanned impromptu question.

[121] Stupid names, I know. Don't blame me, blame the lame cartoon!

you can improve your weakness or if you should outsource this grief to someone else. Team up with someone whose skills compliment your own. Help each other go farther than either of you could alone.

Feel free to fail.

Failure is not always as bad as we make it out to be. We can learn from it, discover new priorities, push our creative limits and make us realize a new world of possibilities. Failure is one of the more important steps in succeeding. It tells us something we thought would work doesn't work and pinpoints what's important in our plan, since we can't succeed until we fix it.

Look over every failure. Identify the working parts and focus on the broken pieces. Soon you'll be failing less and less, learning as you go. Everyone talks about how important education is right? Why not take this opportunity to learn something immediately applicable instead of wasting all that money on someplace overpriced like Harvard, Yale or the New Hampshire Technical Institute.

Listen to a complainer.

They're not hard to find. Sit one down and let them go crazy. Listen contemplatively, trying to look at their side of the issue. Do they have valid points? Without adding their personality into the equation, does what they say make sense? Often we overlook nuggets of useful information because it's swirling around in the toilet of their personality.

It's good practice for identifying problems. It's also good to work on your insincere "Sincerity Face." At some point you'll run into someone who is what we call "bat-shit crazy."[122] You're still going to have to

---

[122] It's a technical term, you hear it in places of higher education, but it's a real condition.

deal with them as well. If you can perfect the "Sincerity Face," you just might survive the encounter unscathed.

Start looking up information.

You're going to hear a lot of rumors, lies and misinformation in your lifetime, so now's the time to practice looking up information. You can go on the interwebs[123] or even a library.[124] Inside are lots and lots of books. Maybe even some microfiche.[125] If there is something you don't believe, start doing some research. You may learn more than you thought!

Practice saying "No."

Get used to saying it out loud instead of in your head whenever you actually say "yes." Give yourself the freedom to choose your actions without feeling obligated to someone else all the time. We all have obligations that we need to fulfill, though not every request of our time needs to be a commitment.

At first you'll probably say "no", then immediately follow it up with some lame excuse as to why you can't, how horrible you feel because you can't and then you may relent and say "yes". Over time and with a bit of practice, you'll get the hang of it. Saying "no" will come quite easily. Just remember to use it at the right moments. You can still get in to trouble now and then if you use it at the wrong time.[126]

---

[123] I hear it's a series of tubes!

[124] That's the building that the homeless use to pee in and keep warm in the winter.

[125] Secret: They're not really fish!

[126] Like disobeying the police during an arrest, defying a direct order while in the military or anytime your wife asks you to do something.

Set out some goals you want to accomplish.

Try not to limit yourself until we start the process of asking ourselves "why?" Why do you want the goal? What's going to stop you from achieving this goal?

Often we mislabel our goals because what we want is disguised as something else. We want to be rich. Why? Because we want a stable environment for our family. Do you need to be rich to do that?

No…but it doesn't hurt, does it?[127]

Stop putting heavy expectations on yourself.

List out what your expectations are. Not your goals but your expectations. Are they realistic? Who put these expectations in your head? Family? Work? Yourself?

Life is tough enough without trying to be perfect or do something some way that someone else wants you to do it.[128]

Almost anyone can apply negative thinking into their lives. For my last example, I'll use a fictional character that I feel boils down negative thinking for positive results.

Ladies and gentleman, I give you Batman!

Let me say this before I get started: I am not advocating vigilantes!

I'll use the Caped Crusader to highlight how his negative thinking has benefited not only him but Gotham City as a whole.

127 Am I right? Can I hear all the rich people say "Amen!"? HOLLA! - Ok, that didn't sound as cool as I thought it would before I wrote it.

128 I mean, look at how confusing that sentence was to read, now try it in real life! Dizzying, isn't it?

Admitting there's a problem – Batman only came into existence when Gotham started going down the tubes. Bruce Wayne[129] realized the police were either unable to wouldn't fix the crime problem for various reasons. Batman saw a place for improvement and went to town.

Never settling, always improving – Batman is always looking at his costume for flaws, areas of weakness that he can improve on. Can't move your head, ask Lucius Fox to fix it. Worried about dog bites? Get Lucius to improve the armor. Positive thinking can cause complacency. If you like something, you don't see a need to make it better. Negative thinking has always pushed innovation and improvements.

Seeing negative outcomes before they happen – Why wear a mask? To protect the people he cares about. Batman knows that if he were to show his face, everyone he's ever known and cared about becomes a target.[130]

You can't do it all yourself – Batman always has help. Alfred, Lucius Fox, Commission Gordon, Robin, the Justice League of America. He's not a one man wrecking crew, he has support and he needs that support to do what he does.

The Bat symbol – Batman has even used our natural negativity bias to give him an edge. Knowing the innate fear many people hold of bats, he uses the imagery to gain a psychological advantage.

But this is a comic book, Craig.

---

[129] Spoiler: He's Batman!

[130] Also, wearing it gives Christian Bale an excuse to use his Clint Eastwood impression.

I get it. We all can't be multibillionaire playboy vigilantes. For starters, I am not in any kind of shape. Amorphous lump is NOT a shape. I get winded sleeping.

I don't have the bankroll necessary, either. While I make a good living, I can't go around wasting money on a Kevlar suit and weapons…I've got a business to run!

I have a pretty busy travel schedule. I have enough trouble with my travel suitcase that holds a few dress shirts and a suit, how would I tote my superhero costume around? Try walking through airport security with a cape and gauntlets. You thought taking off your shoes was an issue. Plus, witty cutting sarcasm isn't a superpower… though I feel it should be classified as such.

I also have too much of an ego to have a secret identity. I would be too busy doing the talk show circuit to save people. Unless criminals attack the Today Show, I wouldn't be too much help.

Let's take something a little more realistic. How about tech support?

Let's face it, tech support is an industry built on negativity. Have you ever met an IT person? Negativity is their life blood. There entire job is either fixing problems or preventing problems. Just think about the things you may have installed on your personal computer. For some of you this suddenly got very uncomfortable didn't it? I'll move on…

Do you have antivirus software? You better. It stops seventeen-year-old college students who don't have anything better to do than create a program that will destroy your computer from ruining your life.[131]

---

[131] *Most likely they're doing it for extra credit in Computer Lab.*

Ever hear of a Firewall? They prevent hackers from getting into your files and learning about all the porn sites you visit that you thought no one would ever find out about. Uh…forget I said that. I mean, it prevents them from getting vital information from your computer like credit card info, social security numbers and passwords so they can steal your identity.[132]

Even something as simple as a Surge protector is negative thinking working for you to prevent equipment from frying. Mass storage to prevent all those digital pictures you take from going *poof*. Simple things like "auto save" for Word, so you don't lose information if you forget to save your documents.

{ Positive hammers and negative screwdrivers

You have the tools to be successful right this moment.

I'll let you in on a little secret: You had the tools before you even read this book.[133] You've always had the tools sitting right in front of you all the time. Your body, your mind have been designed to survive and succeed. Why do you think humans inhabit nearly every corner of the globe? Human beings are success machines. Cultures are what divert you from your true self. You have been told not to listen to that inner

---

[132] *And you thought no one would ever want to be you…ha*

[133] *I know what you are thinking: "Why didn't you say this in the introduction?!"*

voice because other people[134] think "negative thoughts" are useless. Thoughts are not useless: they warn us, push us, enlighten us, protect us and inspire us. Only if you listen to them. You don't have to act on every thought you have. Take the time to listen to what they are saying and ask yourself why you are having them.

This is why, as my farewell gift to you,[135] I am giving you permission.

Permission to listen to your negative thoughts.

You're going to have them whether you want them or not, so take a second to reflect on what those thoughts really mean. I like to think of negative thoughts in the same way we think of insulin. Insulin, like negative thinking, is a natural product of our bodies. We need it to survive and be healthy. Too much or too little insulin will cause us great health concerns. With the right amounts we are at peak performance.

Negative thinking is the same. Ignore it and you fall into traps you could have avoided. Embrace it too much and you feel overwhelmed, anxious and helpless. Balanced with a positive attitude and you have a powerful tool at your disposal, one that many people are telling you to ignore despite it being a natural part of the human thought process.

Stop feeling guilty that you're not the bundle of sunshine the world tells you that you "should" be. As someone prepared to face failure, the odds of actually failing become less. Being prepared, planning ahead, and avoiding obstacles. These are all great things as you move

---

[134] You know who they are.

[135] Not really a gift, you did have to pay for the book.

through life. Stop closing your eyes and hoping and start opening your mind up to the reality of the moment.

Are all negative thoughts good for you? Of course not. Just like all positive thoughts are not productive or useful. This is why you take an honest, reasonable look at any thought you have.

OBLIGATORY SELF-REFERENTIAL QUOTE FROM THE AUTHOR

"Start playing the hand that you've been dealt instead of wishing for more aces."

CRAIG PRICE (THAT'S ME!)

An ounce of prevention is worth more than a pound of cure. Just like a few moments of reflection is worth more than the time spent fixing a problem you could have avoided.

Negativity is just another tool. You can choose to use it or not. If you are an overwhelmingly diehard positive person, good for you. Stay that way if you like.

Hopefully you've gained some insight on why the rest of us aren't as cheery. Maybe you have a little more understanding from the other side of the coin.

If you're a negative leaning thinker, rejoice! This is an affirmation that you're doing fine. You thought you had the answers before, now you *know*.

We know attitude doesn't predict results. Stop focusing on the attitude and focus on the results.

Think about it as putting pictures on a wall. You've got all these pictures you want to hang on the wall, so you head to your toolbox. Since we've been conditioned to be positive, we're going to look for a positive hammer. We're looking through the box and instead of a positive hammer we find a negative screwdriver.

Can you hang a picture on a wall with a screwdriver? Of course you can. Just ask my wife. When we first moved into our house, she couldn't wait to hang some artwork and photos on the wall. She looked around and couldn't find a hammer. Instead she found a big fat-handled screwdriver. She used the fat handle to hammer in all the nails for her pictures.

Of course the screwdriver now looks like the dogs have chewed on it, but where are the pictures? On the wall.

When it comes down to it, isn't that all we're trying to do on a daily basis? Just get the pictures on the wall the best way we know how? It doesn't matter *how* you do it, be it hammer, screwdriver or as my wife would tell me later "I used the screwdriver because I couldn't find any stiletto heels." It's a matter of *if* you get it done.

It's the same with how you think. If the best way to figure something out for you is using negative thinking, use it. If it's positive thinking, go for it!

If there is a person in your office you see being negative, use that to help the office. Don't punish the person for their natural tendencies. Don't ignore them; they may have the answer you're looking for.

You have the tools regardless of your attitude, regardless of your disposition.

Success happens for the good, the bad, the nice, the mean, the stingy and the charitable.

There is no one way of doing anything.

Maybe you've read this entire book and think I'm full of crap. That maybe this won't work for you. That's fine with me. At least you're making an informed decision. The key is to find what works for you, not what others say should work.

The common component is hard work, reason and flexibility. If you have those things or partner yourself up with people who do, there is no excuse why you can't ultimately be successful.

I'm positive about that.

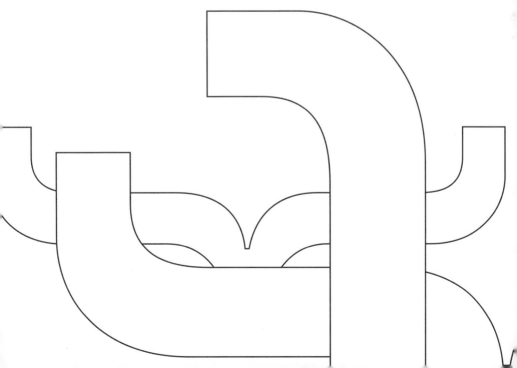

ABOUT THE AUTHOR

A realist by nature and a professional speaker, consultant, entertainer by trade, Craig[136] has worked with some of the most effective and diverse corporate leaders, from multibillion-dollar manufacturers to top universities, around the country. He has a background in customer service, entertainment, telecommunications, and safety. A former professional stand-up comedian, Craig won the coveted title of "Houston's Funniest Person." He is also an actor with television, voice-over and national radio program experience. He lives in Houston with his understanding wife and two remarkably lazy dogs.

To learn more about Craig, or if you are interested in having him present at your next conference, association meeting or corporate event, contact him below:

Craig Price c/o Price Points
2400 McCue, Suite #443 Houston, TX 77056
Office: 877.572.7890 - Direct: 281.546.1664
craig@speakercraigprice.com www.speakercraigprice.com

---

[136] I know, I look like a sickly magician. But now you know which Craig Price wrote it.

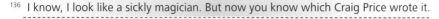